The Third Coming of Spiritual Liberation

A historical perspective that examines the origin of contemporary elitists' mass control as opposed to individuals seeking mental and spiritual liberation.

By

Khå Maa Hetep

Khå Maa Hetep

Bronx, New York

Khå Maa Hetep
750 Baychester Ave
Bronx, NY, 10475
www.thethirdcoming.com

Publisher's Note: This is a work of nonfiction. Names, characters, places, and incidents are a product of socio-religious narratives, and historical and/or contemporary events. Locales and public names are used for historical and contemporary significance. Resemblance to actual people, living or dead, or to businesses, companies, events, institutions, or locales is intentional.

The Third Coming of Spiritual Liberation/ Khå Maa Hetep . . . 1st ed
ISBN: 978-0-578-98309-7

This book is dedicated to my wife, Tena Sa Ba Seshua-t, members of Ausar Auset Society International, and the History and English Departments at Bronx Health Sciences High School. My wife, Tena Sa Ba Seshua-t, has stood by my side throughout this entire authorship process. She serves as encouragement, as we engage in healthy discussions articulated throughout this literature. The African centered, spiritual concepts, culture, and lifestyle mentioned within this text are actualized and lived among members of Ausar Auset Society International, led by the honorable, Dr. Ra Un Nefer Amen. Discourse with the History and English Departments at Bronx Health Sciences High School has also assisted with developing thematic, historical, and scientific concepts, leading to further structural editing to produce this final product.

"It always seems impossible until it is done."
Nelson Mandela

CONTENTS

Author's Preface 8

Introduction 11

Non-Western Holistic Spiritual Culture and Religion 11

Chaperter One Love and Spiritual Liberation or Fear and Socio-religious Control 13

Traditional African Practices for Spiritual and Physical Liberation 16

Chapter Two Positive-Spiritual Initiation to Cultivate Love 21

The Image and Likeness of The Supreme Creator Being 24

Chapter Three For Mass Control, Media Programs the Mind and Spirit with Fear and Consumerism 28

Indiscriminate Assimilation into Societies that Promote Fear and Mindless Consumerism: A Means of Distraction and Control 33

Propagation of Institutionalized Miseducation in Exclusive Support of Strict Evolutionary Theory 38

Chapter Four Patriarchy: An Insatiable, Greco-Roman Desire to Dominate and Control Others 42

Greco-Roman and Caucasian Methodology of Mass Subjugation 47

The Consumption of a Lead-Based Substance Called Sapa.. 50

A Nationalistic Tradition of Writing Texts that Celebrates War and Conquest 54

Chapter Five To Consolidate Power and to be Venerated as a God, Emperor Constantine Organizes a New Socio-religious Syncretism 58

The Vision of the Cross: Edits to Constantine's Official Biography 62

The 325 CE Council of Nicaea 64

Chapter Six The Veneration of Mithras.............................. 69

Mithraism: A Precursor to Syncretic Roman Catholicism and Organized Christianity.. 73

Chapter Seven Ritualized Blood Sacrifice: To Control Others Through Fear.. 79

Asiatic or Persian, and Greco-Roman Occupation of Ancient Egypt (Kemet): A Perversion of African Knowledge of Creation and Purpose.. 83

Chapter Eight Trance Induction to Supplicate the Spiritual Realm for Assistance.. 87

Ausarianism, Mithraism, Catholicism, and Christianity....... 89

Krishna, Conventional Science, and God's Consciousness .. 94

Chapter Nine Maya: In Opposition to Nurturing and Cherishing Eternal Peace and Joy 100

Accessing Knowledge and Information Stored in DNA to Restore Ancient, Spiritual Magnificence.......................... 108

Spiritual Traditions in Common Among Eastern, African, and Western Societies 110

Chapter Ten Systemic Programming to Indoctrinate Negativity, While Inhibiting Connections to Spiritual Reality and Truth....... 114

Cognitive Dissonance and Maya...................................... 118

Metaphysical and Spiritual Experiences: Pushing the Margins of Conventional Science for Explanations of Destiny........ 120

Chapter Eleven Thousands of Years Before Christ: A Metaphysical Lifestyle Initiates Women and Men into an Ausarian (Osiris) Elevated Consciousness 123

Resurrection and Rebirth of the Divine Self: Ausar........... 130

Chapter Twelve Divinity is The Will to Choose to Make Correct, Conscious Decisions 134

Causes of Distortion that Inhibit Lifestyle Choices Aligned to God's Will: Heru Faculty 137

Well Informed Thorough Research to Positively Impact the Heru Faculty: The Will and the Freedom to Choose 139

Chapter Thirteen Societies that Promote Detachment from the Neteru (Nature) and God's Divine laws 144

Speaks for Itself and Stands on Its Own: Rudyard Kipling's Poetry 148

Heru: An Ancestral Understanding of the Freedom to Choose to be Always Peaceful and Joyful.................................... 150

Chapter Fourteen African Civilizations are the Oldest and Most Spiritually Evolved 156

The Shaft of Ausar (Osiris): The Father of Heru (Horus)... 159

Chapter Fifteen Deceptive Machinations and Concoctions of the Mind for Mass Control 166

Truth Verified by History: Live Divinity as the Daughters and Sons of God 171

Chapter Sixteen Mental and Spiritual Liberation are not Found by Assimilation into Societies that Promote Sycophantic Acceptance 175

Abrahamic Lifestyle of the Sycophant: Inhibition of Mass Mental and Spiritual Liberation.. 177

Chapter Seventeen In the Beginning There Was Consciousness 181

The Nicene Creed: A Solution to the Arius Controversy at the 325 CE Council of Nicaea 184

Chapter Eighteen Eurocentric Spiritual Evolution: Methodologies to Incarnate Christ's Holy Spirit............... 187

An Emphasis on Physical Evolution................................ 190

Chapter Nineteeen Sons and Daughters of Men Who Identify with Original Sin 192

Negative Emotionalism.. 194

Chapter Twenty Black Africans: The Original Anatomical and Spiritually Evolved Modern Humans (Homo sapien sapiens) 197

Y Chromosome Adam: A Black African 199

Chapter Twenty-one The Daughters and Sons of God: The Paut Neteru and Metu Neter 202

Divisions of the Spirit 204

Chapter Twenty-two The Sahu and Ab Divisions of the Spirit 208

Chapter Twenty-three The Shekhem, Khu and Ba Divisions of the Spirit 211

Conclusion 215

BIBLIOGRAPY TO CHAPTERS 217

Author's Preface

To stay relevant, governments of today illicit support and sustain mass control, by proposing that one of its essential functions is to protect citizens from foreign terror attack. Similarly, Abrahamic socio-religious institutions promote that its purpose is to insulate congregants from Satan's temptation and terrorizing hellfire. Fear and ignorance do not liberate the spirit and mind to assist citizens with becoming critical thinkers, who are not bound, gagged, and tube fed by governments, or Abrahamic institutions. Historical records show that governments are wedded to, and work hand in glove with religious organizations. For mass control, the pairing of government with organized, Abrahamic religions is made clear as intense descriptive language, violent-media imagery, and iconographic symbolism of human sacrifice are used to cause psychological and spiritual stagnation, where citizens and congregants are confined within a fear-based reality.

The iconographic symbolism of human sacrifice illustrates the physical end of the first coming of Christ Jesus through crucifixion. As discussed in this text, the phrase, or possible reality of the second coming of Jesus is also rather ambiguous and obtuse. Since the second coming is illusive, uncertain, or transient, the third coming as mentioned in the title, is not the return of Jesus, but is the aspiration to arouse and awaken the divine Christ that lives within humankind.

Written mainly by men of the Abrahamic, socio-religious persuasion and Eurocentric, White supremacist ideology, textbooks in Western academia also uphold the racists' agenda that the advent of civilization occurred approximately 5,000 years ago. Science researchers and historians use the location of fossilized remains and DNA evidence to document and share information that modern humans or Homo sapien sapiens evolved and emerged in Africa, approximately 250,000 to 290,000 years ago. Writing systems and a sedentary lifestyle are pivotal to the Eurocentric definition of civilization. As much as Caucasians or Greco-Romans take credit for the formation of civilization, Homer's Iliad and Odyssey were written only in the 8th century BCE. In contrast, Eurocentric history textbooks report that civilization began approximately 6,000 years ago in Sumer, Mesopotamia with Asian people having aquiline features.

Their biased and contradictory analysis suggests that before civilization could develop, 250,000-year-old Black Africans, or Homo sapien sapiens had to interbreed, and evolve into people with the Asian phenotype, who are more intelligent. This biased interpretation of modern humans' physical and spiritual evolution also blatantly implies that for approximately 244,000 years, Black Africans were mindless beasts, wandering the Earth, worshiping graven images and idols of their ancestors, and creator gods in the Sun, wind, and rain. Historical Eurocentric analysis also suffers from selective amnesia by forgetting to include 12,000-year-old megalithic civilizations, such as Gobekli Tepe in modern day Turkey. At this location, chiseled into megaliths, there are symbols and images that link the ancient people of Gobekli Tepe with that of indigenous Black, Africans of Australia. As the research of Mr. Robert M. Schoch suggests, the Gobekli Tepe megalithic symbols and images are forms of writing, pictographs, and narration. Moreover, the native, indigenous people of Australia did not refer to themselves as aboriginals, which is a pejorative term used by English colonizers. An historical and etymological analysis of the name aboriginal suggests a genocidal hatred of indigenous, original people, as the prefix abhor is used in this disparaging moniker.

Introduction

Non-Western Holistic Spiritual Culture and Religion

In general, to control and limit humankind to a purely empirical reality that is restricted by observations made by the five senses and instrumentation, the Holy Bible as well as other spiritual texts have been misinterpreted to play critical roles in shaping and establishing the dominance of geopolitical business, banking, and socio-religious leadership. This goal of establishing dominance to limit and control humankind, which can begin with religion, creates ideological, as well as physical or tangible contradictions. In simple terms, religion and the practice of spirituality are presumed to bring liberating experiences of mind, body, and soul. Instead of experiencing altered states of heightened reality through prayer and meditation, the controlling influence of fearmongering attempts to confine individuals within the materialistic trappings of negative emotionalism.

Without any obligation to commit to a spiritual lifestyle, the quid pro quo is to support specific religious organizations with monetary contributions, and in return, receive material blessings. Often in contrast to this philosophy of indulgences or payment to possibly experience spiritual liberation, non-Abrahamic text and traditions do provide instructions for lifestyle changes to access greater forms of mental freedom through practices to enhance clairvoyant abilities. Some of these texts include Hinduism's Vedas, Buddhism's Tripiṭaka and Dhammapada, and Taoist's writing of Dao De Jing, Lau Tzu, and the I Ching oracle system. The etymology of religion, Abrahamic and otherwise, means connecting or reuniting people with God, similar to a ligament that ties bone to bone. In other words, practitioners of spirituality and even religion should manifest experiences of liberation, as well as eternal peace and joy.

Unlike the controlling influence of global leadership and governments, Eastern and African esoteric societies cherish and share ancient, but practical-spiritual systems that can help adherents attain forms of divine liberation. However, Taoist and certain Buddhist sects can be labeled as atheistic. They still practice spiritual or energy enhancing rituals to elevate their consciousness above that of the average controlled or slumbering human. Through learned methodologies applied using the science of consciousness elevation, practitioners arouse internal energies. This, in turn, stimulates physical, spiritual, and psychic awareness to such elevated levels that practitioners can be described as divine, peaceful, and loving, while walking among emotionally controlled humans on this physical plane of existence.

Chapter One

Love and Spiritual Liberation or Fear and Socio-religious Control

Historically, one method by which elites maintained physical control over certain groups of people was by kidnapping Africans into perpetual, chattel slavery. In contemporary societies, an aspect of this protracted effort of control – physical, mental, and psychic – displays itself through historic attempts to negate, minimize, and distance humankind from the spiritually liberating practices and power of Africans. In the past, the brutal, harsh, and inhuman treatment of chattel slaves was a means of instilling fear into the human psyche. In conjunction with labeling the ancient-traditional practices of Africans as being evil, and belonging to devil worshipers, brutality serves to impact negatively and distance humankind from the progenitors of spiritual science. This elitists' systematic method of ill-treatment and stereotypical, negative labeling continues to exert adverse effects on Africans and Blacks throughout the diaspora, as well as humankind in general. The label of evil, Voodoo practitioner and devil worshiper causes most people to distance themselves from the spiritual traditions and customs of former chattel-slave populations.

Written into specific Old Testament and other nationalistic texts, as justification for theft and genocide perpetrated against polytheistic pagans (pigmented people), monotheistic, zealot soldiers carry out a divine edict or command from God. Similarly, in the contemporary era, adherence to incorrect belief assumes the form of subtly claiming that it is an edict and command from God for monotheists to war against each other: Jews-vs-Christians-vs-Muslims in the Middle East, and elsewhere, as they occupy disputed land and steal natural resources. All spiritual cultures know that there is only one Supreme Being. Still, elitists label groups of people as evil pagans and polytheists, as opposed to righteous monotheists, who worship the only true God. Divisive rhetoric, philosophies, and religious dogma, as well as military conquest, serves to fragment the species, as elites continue to reap illegitimate material rewards and physical benefits.

Just the same, to maintain a semblance of order and control by instilling fear into the human psyche and consciousness, domineering socio-religious and geopolitical groups born out of oppressive, colonial governments have transitioned to form and function within neo-colonial societies. As justification for African, chattel-slave atrocities, this socio-religious and political agenda of dominance, in turn, dispenses false Biblical narratives that correlate African Blacks, as well as those of the diaspora, with being the cursed descendants of Noah's son, Ham. Oddly enough, only the Abrahamic blood of Jesus and Mohammed can save wretched, demonic, and sinful Africans from Ham's curse. However, conventional scholarship speaks to the contrary as mentioned by Felicia R. Lee, who authored a 2003 *New York Times* article entitled "*From Noah's Curse to Slavery's Rationale.*" In this article, Ms. Lee quotes George M. Fredrickson, who says: as for Ham, "It's been a flexible curse – Jews, peasants, and Tatars, have been considered cursed over the years." According to specific scholars and honest academicians, Ham's curse does not discriminate due to consorting with the devil, or by race (phenotypic characteristics), but rather by class, socioeconomic status, or simple misfortune. Mr. Fredrickson, emeritus professor of history at Stanford University, is also the author of "*Racism: A Short History.*"

From the 1400s to 1800s, in many regions of the colonized world, such as Haiti, Jamaica, Brazil, and the American Southern states, African slave populations outnumbered Europeans and their planter class. Thus, Caucasians lived in perpetual fear of slave uprisings, which threatened the lives of the slaveholding gentry, and their supporters. This system of African-chattel slavery was overwhelmingly supported by ignorant middle-class, as well as poor Europeans, who lacked political and socio-economic power to gain access to the opulent lifestyle of the slave-owning gentry. Throughout the different socio-economic levels of Caucasian daily life, from the slave-owning gentry to those living in poverty, ignorance and fear were promoted as the major control method. To secure their position of physical power, European nobility, and the elite-planter class throughout the Americas and Caribbean, masterminded a colonial, socio-political and economic apparatus that functioned within institutionalized systems of government. In this mercantile and capitalist framework, most poor and middle-class Caucasians were the minions inflicting war of total terror on a perpetual class of subjugated Africans. In the Americas, these very same people formed groups of slave catchers, whose job was to capture and return fugitive slaves for a bounty. This oppressive practice intended to hold Blacks in perpetual servitude, later gave rise to the contemporary police state, with law enforcement in support of systemic White supremacy.

Traditional African Practices for Spiritual and Physical Liberation

In colonized regions such as Haiti, Brazil, and Jamaica, to name a few, institutionalized atrocities motivated enslaved Africans to escape to fertile, mountainous areas to form rebellious Maroon societies. In addition to physically freeing themselves by escaping to Maroon encampments, Africans engaged in spiritual rituals and armed struggle for the liberation of other Blacks existing within the atrocities of slavery. They also mobilized ongoing, successful slave revolts, including the Haitian revolution for liberty and independence lasting from 1791 through 1804. To deter captive Africans from these successful, spiritual-revolutionary actions for liberty, the planter class relied on their Caucasian version of Christianity, which Black people were forcefully assimilated into, as a means to demonize, ostracize, and vilify revolution and freedom as the work of devils.

All European nations that warred against each other are today allied through Abrahamic religion and an insatiable desire for military and socio-economic dominance. However, Haiti, the symbolic beacon of successful enslaved African revolution for liberty is forced to pay the highest socio-economic and political price: American, French, and Canadian exploitation and oppression. Abusive action by neo-colonialists' is intended to perpetuate the myth that Haiti and its people are the cursed seed of the devil, because they revolted successfully against the three major colonial powers: France, England, and Spain. Ms. Lee quotes Mr. Braudes, who in a paper for a Yale conference says: "In 18th and 19th century Euro-America, Genesis 9:18-2 became the curse of Ham, a foundation myth for collective degradation, conventionally trotted out as God's reason for condemning generations of dark-skinned peoples from Africa to slavery." More reasonably, Ham's curse of condemnation was not dispensed at the hands of God or Noah. Instead, it is a rationale that soothes the mind of European Judeo-Christians, along with Muslim Arab, Persian, and Ottoman enslavers, in search of an escape from karma.

In the 17th and 18th centuries, Africans were not the only group being kidnapped, ransomed, or held hostage as slaves. During the late 1700s, before and after the American war for independence, the U.S. lacked a navy to protect its merchant ships from the so-called Moors, or Arab, Ottoman, and corsair pirates scouring the Barbary coast of Morocco, Algeria, Tunisia, and Libya. American merchant ships were often sieged by Ottomans, or today's Turkish people, who held Caucasian sailors captive for ransom. Caucasians were then transported to the Middle East and sold into chattel slavery. In the early stages of nationhood, the U.S. paid $80,000 tribute to the Barbary pirates. However, Americans were still harassed by corsair extortionists. Beginning in 1801, theft, piracy, and Caucasian enslavement prompted the U.S. to form a naval unit to battle against the Barbary pirates, as memorialized in the military hymn, celebrating victory in 1805 at the shores of Tripoli, Libya.

Clearly, equal opportunity abusers do not discriminate as they wield physical power and mental control over others. Africans and Blacks of the diaspora should be cognizant and consider the historical perspective of indiscriminate abuse and atrocities against those who are spiritually cultivated, but lacking in sophisticated-military technology. The study and research of history and psychology may bring Africans and Blacks of the diaspora to understand symptoms of psychosis, such as the Stockholm Syndrome, or capture bonding. After their release, victims of oppression and servitude, such as chattel slaves, often continue to identify and empathize with their abusers. Instead of victims blaming themselves, thereby continuing this protracted cycle of oppression, spiritual affinity and connection to African ancestry will reveal that those with political and socio-economic power, and governments are culpable, since they institutionalized perpetual African-chattel slavery. Positive-communication rituals invoke the energies of loving and caring ancestors, who inform and share information to elevate consciousness and the human condition to that of peaceful and joyful divinity.

For fear of being labeled as polytheistic, devil worshipers or Voodoo practitioners, and to be more readily accepted into Western societies – most being major players who gain exorbitant physical wealth from the colonization of Africa – Black people, in general have assimilated the definition of happiness, as the accumulation of quantifiable material possessions. Accelerated assimilation into Western societies also helps avoid being ostracized and vilified for practicing or being acquainted with a traditional and spiritual lifestyle. By distancing themselves from a more traditional way of life that celebrates African and Eastern ancestry, materially endowed pigmented people may be more readily accepted by mainstream societies, instead of being shunned as pariahs, lacking in quantifiable material possessions.

Other than skin color, another physical or empirical criterion employed to inflict injustice is traditional garb or clothing, which can be associated with a religious lifestyle, such as African animism, Hinduism, Buddhism, or Islam. In the contemporary era, biased and corporate-controlled media projects negative images from marginally investigated incidents labeled as acts of terror. Detailed and thorough research of political or government funding of state-sponsored terrorism is barely investigated in mainstream media. The Hegelian dialectic philosophy and its more pervasive school of thought can be linked with government false-flag operations. The genesis of certain political action is philosophical thought and planning, but the result is to affect or influence forceful government policies that restrict, and disregard civil liberties. The Hegelian dialectic works as follows: To maintain control, the government creates the problem, then seemingly implements political solutions at the expense of civil liberty and justice.

Government maintains its relevance and mass control by impacting people who are consumed with thoughts of fear and terror, so they sacrifice individual liberty to gain the illusion of security, freedom, and happiness. Ultimately, government action is at the root of acts of terror from which it benefits by enforcing laws that restrict personal liberty. Acts of terror are used to promote fear, so that people further rationalize and accept mass control, which infringes on personal privacy through government surveillance, as documented by Edward Snowden.

Furthermore, to their materialistic advantage, deception at the hands of elites often deludes and unifies mass populations through religion, which can have the intended purpose of stealing and amassing territory rich in natural resources, during times of war. Nationalism and religion work together to program mass consciousness by manipulating people to fight and die over dribble, scraps, and a corrupt understanding of liberty. Very early in life, subliminal, nationalistic programing takes the form of pledging to fight and die for the flag and country. The same is true of organized, xenophobic religion that promotes the nonsensical oxymoron of God's chosen people and holy wars. Again, contrived by ruling elites so that they can continue their methods of mass control, there is this deceptive understanding of God's purpose for creating life, as well as an illusionary description of acquiring liberty through means of war. From the elitists' perspective, this is supreme, since it also suits their incendiary definition of divinity, and satisfies their role as warmongering gods of this Earth. For people who may participate in traditional, spiritual rituals to achieve clarity and clairvoyance, this deceptive system of physical and empirical control is rather insidious and unsustainable.

Chapter Two

Positive-Spiritual Initiation to Cultivate Love

Due to the required dedication and devotion to the science of consciousness elevation, African practitioners and others may be perceived as esoteric, or a unique and exotic challenge to be understood. An esoteric lifestyle is rather abstract and calls for extensive hours of internal inquiry. The practice of searching within for answers by slowing the breath, and the flow of thoughts entering awareness also tends to elevate consciousness to reveal government and global leadership's true nature. By adhering to occult principles, humankind can hereafter gain greater insight into the ideological and physical or tangible divide between control versus spiritual liberation. The most fascinating yet subtle aspect of specific esoteric teachings is that by practicing biochemical and electromagnetic energy manipulation techniques, such as Qi Gong, processing information and experiences through limited five senses and instrumentation takes the background, while developing enhanced awareness and intuitive ability comes to the foreground to bring about spiritual growth and power.

An essential understanding of truly spiritual practices is that strict empirical and atheistic interpretations of natural phenomena, such as in Western academia, stands in opposition to traditional lifestyles from Eastern and African regions. Spiritual practices from these areas can possibly include rituals that incorporate prayer, meditation, yoga, Qi Gong, and hekau (sounds and words of power) to heighten perceptions beyond simple empirical interpretations of the natural world. The integration of certain techniques to elevate psychic or extrasensory abilities and awareness goes beyond the limited scope of empirical assessments of perceived occurrences, which shape superficial perspectives of reality. The practitioner's lifestyle includes spiritual rituals and customs that work to sensitize, stimulate, and arouse dormant extrasensory abilities to generate enhanced experiences of life events, through which divine-ancestral voices are heard. Given the limited scope of empirical analysis, noninitiates sensing these same events in life might interpret them as being blasé and commonplace, since reality is not perceived at the same level of elevated consciousness.

If the masses are ignorant, and through miseducation, are deprived of information about their spiritual anatomy and power, deception can be more effectively dispensed, and control sustained by elites. Another method of dominance is nestled within Abrahamic traditions, which promote the false notion that innate corruption and original sin renders humankind incapable of regulating its less evolved, internal-lower animal. The masses are indoctrinated to believe that they must rely on an external source for self-control and liberation, such as spiritual intermediaries and intercessors, an electronic device of sorts, medication, and even restrictive government institutions. The concern is that enticement through mass media and dependence on external sources for contrived liberation and power can become a means of entanglement, which cannot free the mind, body, and spirit. In simple terms, humankind has been deprived of proper education concerning its origin, purpose, and divinity, which when studied, internalized, and lived, neurological pathways form that reunite the species to God and nature. Clearly, Homo sapien sapiens (modern humans) are being programmed through Eurocentric warmongering and dominance to despise and disrespect nature, presuming that electronic technology can replace their divine connections to The Creator.

In part, due to this current world order that celebrates decadence and depravity, the path of spiritual growth, evolution, and societal change has been inhibited. Although the contemporary era is referred to as the information age, mass populations are saturated with ignorance and degradation, which causes an aversion to spiritual resources that can be studied and practiced to achieve and sustain correct moral behavior. In all instances, enlightenment and self-control can result in proper decisions and actions, which decrease the need for intervention by external, manipulative forces, such as governments. Identification with a pure, enlightened state of divinity could decrease criminal activity and relegate the state or government law enforcement agencies to engage in more magnanimous behavior, since less punishment and more rehabilitation may be required.

The Image and Likeness of The Supreme Creator Being

A truly divine lifestyle that reflects God's likeness, in terms of Its goodness and mercy, has been co-opted and replaced by insensitive, corrupt, and materialistic societies that lack spiritual insight and clairvoyance. Instead of humankind uniting around the shared knowledge that there is only one Supreme Being that is good and pure, assimilation into materialistic societies and elitism takes precedence and motivates people to distance and isolate themselves from the African traditions of former slaves. The fear that discriminatory systems of persecution at the hands of government institutions will, in turn, dispense injustice onto those who have previously assimilated into mainstream society is the driving force.

Most of this entire system of control is based on superficial, empirical evidence which elitists can manipulate. If one group is ignorant, materialistic, empirically minded, and functioning at lower levels of awareness, they can control and manipulate those who function on the same or even lower levels of spiritual existence. When more people begin to compile and synthesize evidence concerning the positive-spiritual philosophies and lifestyle of all, if not most ancient, pigmented cultures, there should be confirmation of attainable higher forms of existence and values that can be emulated. Information from these ancient, spiritual systems can be practiced, internalized, and lived to become knowledge, while experiencing aspects of mental liberation. If the masses were to lift the veil of ignorance through ancient, traditional practices, they would change their behavior and influence governments to work. towards humankind's best interest, instead of an elitist, self-serving minority

Again, due to limited sensibility and sensitivity, noninitiates are unaware and often dispute the existence of energies on higher planes of existence that transition to lower levels for life-affirming communication to assist with the elevation of consciousness. Non-initiates maintain this denial mindset, since they are not receptive to communication from higher levels of positive-spiritual existence. The uninitiated masses are heavily influenced by organized religious, business, banking, and geopolitical leadership who are elitists by nature.

Nuanced within dominant, egotistical, Western thought and philosophy is the concept that one group of people is better than or superior to other groups based on intellectual abilities to develop and enforce policy intended to amass wealth through the oppressive occupation of territory belonging to others. Superiority also takes pseudo-intellectual prowess to manufacture weapons of mass destruction to intimidate and threaten those who do not conform to the nationalistic machinations of those with physical power. These philosophies and actions are intended to overemphasize wealth accumulation as a means to distract, obstruct or deny humankind from searching for, and attaining aspects of spiritual liberation through divinity, divination practices, and ancestral communication rituals.

Due to persistent-negative emotionalism, those who are socialized and assimilated into dominant, Western societies are also precluded from experiencing true spiritual growth and power. As a result, it is challenging for the masses, who are being misled by mainstream media and miseducation, to accept that African-ancestral energies can speak through contemporary initiates, conveying mental liberation messages. In simple terms, the uninitiated masses do not experience meaningful, spiritual liberation, so it is not real to them. Furthermore, they have been programmed through socialization to doubt spiritual encounters stemming from traditions that celebrate African ancestry. They also deny the life-altering peaceful and purposeful, contemporary experiences of African ancestry as messaged and channeled through initiates. To broaden this spectrum of denial, stereotypical media programming and conditioning combined with public systems of miseducation are intended to refute the civilizing contribution of Africans and subsequently reject those of other pigmented people. All of this is to perpetuate the formation of self-serving psychic or mental slaves and captives, driven by the acquisition of material possessions to fulfill the illusion of happiness.

An extension of elitism, beyond that of self-serving leadership, can be expressed by those who falsely believe that, for whatever reasons, they are better than or superior to other members of humankind. In part, due to their feckless obsession with deceiving and controlling others, elitists cultivate negative thoughts, which feed emotions that manifest in actions against their own species and nature. This is in opposition to the ancient traditions of pigmented people, which can help lift the veil of ignorance to reveal higher forms of awareness, thereby making mass control more difficult. Ancient traditions can be described as a positive lifestyle that emulates God's spirit and consciousness, which resides in all things. A lifestyle that is contrary to this truth is to dishonor God and Its creations. As such, all of God's creations, animate, inanimate, subatomic, and microscopic must be acknowledged and respected as organs and components within The Creator's body. Although ancient, pigmented people innately know and experience God's true nature as spiritual liberation, to limit and control humankind, elitists label Eastern and African psychic rituals and practices as being Voodoo, superstition, and occult, which means to see more clearly.

Chapter Three

For Mass Control, Media Programs the Mind and Spirit with Fear and Consumerism

In part, due to the influence of politicized mass-media, citizens are misinformed. This can result in disempowerment by placing trust in government, corporations, and other types of institutions. Other than media potentially being a divisive propaganda tool of deception, there is an elitists' willingness to do and say anything to preserve wealth and positions of perceived power. The phrase *positions of perceived power* is adopted, since most elitists have little self-control over their internal, destructive, negative emotions. Imbalanced-negative emotionalism, if left unchecked, will destroy the individual, as well as those around them. At the root of chattel slavery, the American civil war, and the major world wars is negative emotionalism. Excessive negative emotionalism causes an imbalanced lack of power and influence within the lives of elitists leadership, and this prohibits them from delivering positive societal and personal change. To compensate for this sense of inadequacy and impotence, elitists leadership chooses to wield physical power over others. In turn, elitists begin to think and feel that they are empowered by promoting fear as a means of controlling mass populations, who may display even more ignorance and lack of power over themselves.

Again, politicized mass-media deception results in citizens redirecting individual power of choice, and trust, by misplacing it in the government's hands. Trust is given to corporations and other government institutions, which results in abdicating the personal power of choice. Since it perceives corporate leadership's potential loss of control and influence over mass populations as being disempowering and against its best interests, government will never implement educational policy to facilitate and guide citizens to self-empowerment, as well as balanced and harmonious choices. On the other hand, citizens can empower themselves through due diligence and research to mitigate high levels of media propaganda and misinformation. As a result, of less consequence would be citizens forfeiting their right to avoid products and services from specific corporations and campaign financiers, whose actions negatively impact the ecological balance within global societies. Clearly, in the mind of government and business elitists, it is in their best interest to maintain this plantation of psychic slaves and ignorant citizens, so that physical power and mental control are perpetuated.

Do not be deluded into believing that government, as it currently exists, has positive intentions for its people. Work distractions, family and other life obligations, media deceptions, and false political promises, all function to influence citizens to neglect due diligence and research. Compared to other forms of political and economic systems, mass-media propaganda, and nationalistic conditioning promote the false notion that capitalists and democratic nations are undeniably in favor of physically protecting, and educating its people to be productive, mentally liberated critical thinkers. However, most empirical educational systems that disregard positive, spiritual initiation are intended to shape productive taxpayers, precluded from seeking and acquiring mental liberation and clairvoyance. At a very young age, nationalistic songs and pledges are educational tools to indoctrinate and produce obedient, taxpaying slaves who believe that the state is concerned with, and serves their best interest.

As of 2021, most people, or the common man employed by private or public sectors are taxed at higher rates than elites who formed private businesses and media corporations. However, due to employment obligations, family responsibilities, and lack of leisure and funding, the common man may be excluded from the political arena and the pursuit of public office. Potentially, there can be conscientious, actionable choices that impact the political process. However, most citizens function within a psychic or mental confine that is heavily influenced by media programming. For example, mainstream media does not inform the public about the historical event of fluoridating drinking water and its adverse health effects. A simple suggestion is to research diluting the industrial waste product, fluoride, into public drinking water.

The rationale for this practice is to harden teeth, thereby protecting consumers from tooth decay. Comparatively speaking, most toothpaste brands are already fluoridated, which is more sensible, since it is directly applied for a minute or longer. Also, toothpaste is not meant to be swallowed. On the other hand, the duration of time that consumed-fluoridated water is exposed to teeth can be measured in seconds, instead of minutes. As the adage goes: *Over the teeth, past the gums, look out stomach here it comes* to be absorbed by the digestive system, and other body parts. The chemical, fluoride, consumed in drinking water is absorbed by the body to yield healthier, stronger teeth. Other body systems absorb toxic-fluoridated water, which also calcifies specific areas of vital organs, such as the brain

The possible intent of this government or corporate practice of dumping sodium fluoride into municipal water supplies, may aim to inhibit higher brain function so that people are docile, mindless consumers, obedient to mundane, empirical directions and commands. Regardless of the intent to make obedient, mindless servants, global populations continue to protest the fascist, police state's murder and brutalization of innocent Black people. For the aluminum industry, however, diluting sodium fluoride into municipal water supplies is a viable alternative for getting rid of commercial wastes, instead of bellowing plumes of toxic gas into the atmosphere. Initiate changes in behavior by using filtered, non-fluoridated water to cleanse the mind, body, and spirit which helps elevate consciousness, thereby cultivating shifts in the mental and social paradigm. This cleansing stimulates further behavioral changes, resulting in diminished support and energy given to this corrupt-global system, which deliberately toxifies drinking water to retard higher-mental cognition and extrasensory abilities, and causes other adverse health effects. Also, research websites that send electronic petitions to government officials to stop the practice of fluoridating water.

Again, media plays a major role in creating and fortifying this plantation by ingraining fictitious images and phrases into most people's mind. For example, during media appearances, geopolitical leadership and American politicians often refer to taxpayers' dollars. Media conditioning occurs as follows: Repeat distortions of truth, or lies, until it becomes believable and truthful to the mind, eyes, and imagination of viewers. Due to repetition, a conditioned response occurs, and at that very moment, images of honest and concerned politicians come to bear, although representatives mouthing taxpayers' dollars may care little about constituency concerns. The phrase, taxpayers' dollars, implies that the democratic process can replace politicians, if they do not allocate funding based on educated and informed constituent choices. This elusive philosophy of government obligation to the people functions to serve elitists, who control media and the political process.

Inordinate campaign financing needed to place candidates in office tends to corrupt the democratic political machine. Political obligations are often to campaign financiers instead of the national population. In May of 2017, Ray Gross authored an internet article for the *Billings Gazette.* He says: "The Citizens United US Supreme Court Decision makes it legal for corporations, unions, super PACs, and billionaires to spend as much money as they want to buy elections. This has made dirty politics a lucrative business."

Indiscriminate Assimilation into Societies that Promote Fear and Mindless Consumerism: A Means of Distraction and Control

Mainstream media and public miseducation promote the belief that indiscriminate consumerism in the form of quantifiable physical possessions is proof of upward mobility and successful assimilation into materialistic societies. Most people are unaware and rather nonchalant about the fact that assimilation does not offer spiritual liberation. To the contrary, it provides greater control and increases profit for geopolitical, religious, business, and banking elites who regulate capital, and its means of distribution. Fiat currency is a means of control, since global populations must conform to the dictates and secular laws of those who regulate its production and distribution, such as privatized-central banking and government institutions.

Overtly, geopolitical leaders claim to serve their nation's interest and the wellbeing of humankind, but their financial, business, and religious institutions are elitist and self-serving. The term self-serving can mean that these institutions have been designed and established to serve the desires of those who insert their materialistic, personal self-interest which implicitly shapes government policy. For example, in the U.S., Wall Street, or the financial and banking sector manipulated or was in collusion with government, or geopolitical leadership to deregulate the real estate industry, thereby creating a housing bubble that led to the Great Recession of December 2007 to June 2009. Its negative impact extended well beyond this two-year-period to cause unemployment and property loss, thereby lowering the middle-class quality of life. These are not natural market cycles but are forms of artificial manipulation to create exorbitant wealth for elites.

These superficial and empirical conditions continue to enhance the materialistic lifestyle of the wealthiest 1% through the acquisition of resources and possessions, such as real estate and businesses, lost during recessionary periods. These business cycles are artificial and manipulated to form predatory environments where humans prey on the misfortunes of others. In situations such as this, clearly, the self-serving financial interest of elitists direct government policy, which adversely affects a nation and its people. With the intended purpose of redistributing and gaining greater material wealth, by manipulating those within its sphere of influence, this geopolitical system of mass control is incapable of serving the peoples' best interest, since it is designed to capture and redirect tax revenue and other resources generated by diligent and dedicated citizens, or psychic slaves. To continually increase the material wealth of elites, a perpetual plantation of psychic slaves has been established to harvest the energies of working-class populations, who are confined by lower-spiritual levels of awareness.

Furthermore, the public should fully understand the far-reaching influence of profit-driven, elitists business, banking, and geopolitical leadership. Not broadcasted on CNN or any of the major news channels is taxpayers' dollars spent supporting America's longest war in Afghanistan. During the early months of 2021, U.S. troops still guarded poppy fields from which highly addictive medical opiates, and illegal drugs, such as heroin and opium are derived. The nightly news would say that troops were there to protect the American people from radical Islam and other forms of terrorism. U.S. soldiers were in Afghanistan to protect international pharmaceutical companies' elitist interests, and that of other globally sanctioned drug lords. Global populations remain drugged, comatose, and unable to engender social justice and political change due to low levels of awareness to see past the veil of deception. Seeing past the veil would trigger an understanding that government, as it currently exists, functions to serve those who uphold its corrupt system of biased miseducation, media propaganda, and mass control.

Again, preoccupied, and misinformed citizens adhere to media propaganda that the American military is dispersed worldwide to protect people against radical Islam. This may or may not be the case, however. For certain, based on campaign promises to increase or decrease military spending, citizens vote for a specific presidential candidate or political party. However, after officials are elected, citizens have no real power to influence political decisions. Neither does a political, moral code of justice obligate candidates to attempt, or feign to fulfill campaign promises. According to data released by the National Priorities Project, the U.S. president proposed a $1.15 trillion discretionary budget for 2017, which allocated $622.6 billion or 54% to military spending. This is compared to $31.7 billion or 3% on social security and unemployment. Middle-class citizens are taxed most heavily by the federal government, but their voices to direct spending of hard-earned tax dollars are not heard. In general, the lion's share of government spending is to maintain the wealth and position of ruling elites through wars and military aggression.

Military spending to protect *the American way of life* is linked to the nationalized war cry of *liberty and justice for all.* Both mantras, mottos, or phrases were ultimately coined for mass distraction, deception, and manipulation to fight wars, implicitly designed to increase the physical wealth of corporate and political elites, while consolidating their positions of perceived power and control. A contemporary symbol of this tactic of control through war and fear, or warfare, can take the form of attempting to extend and fortify the border that divides the U.S. from Mexico. The misplaced concept of national security has been weaponized to foment and nurture fear and negative emotionalism within specific groups, namely Caucasians, so that control and the status quo are maintained. Deliberate, focused attention on a border wall is reminiscent of past political strategies that divide America along racial lines by using ill-conceived, socio-economic and crime statistics to demonize pigmented people. For example, to support the notion that Democrats are weak on crime, a 1988 Republican-party commercial stoked American fears by showcasing a furloughed Black man, Willie Horton, who committed murder while on a weekend pass from prison.

Similarly, the official term *war on drugs* became politically popular during the 1980s and 90s, but in truth, this was a policy to criminalize and incarcerate pigmented people of African descent. Explicitly, the political propaganda credo was a *war on drugs*. However, implicitly, it was, and still is a war to dismantle and divide Black communities, while disrupting the family unit through mass incarceration into privatized, for-profit prisons. Evidence of this is as follows: U.S. intelligence and military-industrial agencies and the political establishment were involved in training Central American Contra rebels to grow, process, and traffic cocaine into the U.S. In the classic

Hegelian dialectic style, there was mandatory sentencing for inner-city Blacks, who were scapegoated as the principal agent of the crack-cocaine epidemic. Clearly, historical evidence connects U.S. intelligence agencies that trained Contra rebels to be drug traffickers, with that of increased powered-cocaine flow into America. Scapegoated, inner-city pigmented people (Blacks and Latinos), who possessed 28 grams of crack cocaine, were mandatorily incarcerated for a five-year minimum for the first offense. Meanwhile, it took 500 grams of the more expensive powdered form of cocaine, the drug of choice used by affluent Caucasians, to warrant the same five-year minimum sentence.

More recently, another deception or distraction was that during the 2018 midterm elections, a 10% middle-class tax cut was promised, but never materialized. Clearly, the anti-immigrant wall and the middle-class tax cut are few examples of false political promises to insulate and protect wealthy elites, while gaining votes from delusional and misinformed working-class citizens. As of October 14th, 2019, President Trump made over 13,000 false or misleading claims during 993 days in office, according to the Washington Post fact-checkers Glenn Kessler, Salvador Rizzo, and Meg Kelly. On January 8th, 2021, President Trump was inflicted with COVID-19, which he flaunted as the China virus, fake news, and a Democrat, political party hoax. Oddly enough, a hoax sent the President to Walter Reed hospital and caused the death of over 600,000 Americans, as of June 27, 2021.

Other than the nation's president, another means of distraction is deceptive public education designed to misinform citizens about their true, divine nature and origin. Again, the intent is to mislead the species by having it identify with an emotional and uncontrollable animal nature or spirit. For example, the theory of strict evolution says that, exclusively on the planet Earth, over an approximate three-billion-year period, bacteria evolved into great apes, which then became modern humans or Homo sapien sapiens. This theory is seemingly atheistic and is often promoted in public education, which socializes people to identify with an uncontrollable animal nature or spirit in need of restraint from external forces, such as geopolitical leadership and government. To sustain the relevance of Abrahamic socio-religious institutions, identification with this uncontrollable animal nature is similar to the scriptural, original sin, which is also in need of restraint from government and church leadership.

Propagation of Institutionalized Miseducation in Exclusive Support of Strict Evolutionary Theory

Miseducational systems disregard implications of the panspermia hypothesis and universal life, but emphatically teaches that linear and strict evolutionary processes occurred without extra-planetary intervention, such as comets and asteroids impacting, or seeding Earth with microbial DNA. Strict evolution would also support the theory that this planet is the only place in the universe that sustains life: simple, complex, or otherwise. On the surface, strict evolution is atheistic, at least, and promotes theories such as Homo sapien sapiens evolving directly from great apes. Within nature, homologous anatomical structures exist, but in and of itself, this is not confirmational evidence of a direct, modern human, ancestral lineage to primates. No DNA and fossilized evidence exist or are yet to be found that directly ties humankind to great apes. Thus, the phrase is *missing link.* Atheistic theories are presumed to be rational, but also subtly promote that modern humans should identify with the limited, emotional animal and primate from which it evolved. As well, animals are labeled as lacking self-control and restraint since they are wild and instinctive. Therefore, animals and humans must be caged and controlled, further supporting the need for intervention from government agencies and other external entities.

Although only 13.4% of America, media stereotypes in popular culture, along with institutionalized racism and systemic miseducation, continues to criminalize Blacks to the extent that they are 40% of the prison population. Media stereotypes are numerous. To describe a few: D. W. Griffth's, 1915 film, *Birth of a Nation* makes Black men into savage-slave caricatures, in uncontrollable bloodlust to rape White women. Fast forward to 1972; there are the *Superfly* movies that glamorize sex trafficking, drug dealing, and the renowned gangster lifestyle. Numerous, as well in history books, there is the noble Black savage, carrying a shield and spear, while dressed in a loincloth diaper, standing on African shores, awaiting arrival of Christian-Caucasian saviors, civilizers, and masters. History books also place the origin of writing and civilization in Mesopotamia's Fertile Crescent in Southeast Asia. Meanwhile, overlooked are the numerous African cultures that had writing and civilization before Mesopotamia and Sumer. Evidence of ancient African migration and global populations are conveniently made irrelevant. However, remains of 4,500-year-old sailing ships exist, similar to the one that is 18 meters, or 59.1 ft. long in an ancient tomb (mastaba) in Abusir (Abu-Sir), Egypt (Kemet). Then, again, conventional history books are duplicitous and deceptive, carrying out geographical illusion and mind games. Ancient Egypt (Kemet) is removed from continental Black Africa and placed in the Middle East, or Levant, and Oriental Asia.

Nonetheless, encoded into African DNA is an innate, diasporic spirituality also known in contemporary America as soul – music, art, dance, and culture – which are means of expression, indicating that Black people are a conduit, experiencing closer connections to nature, through the rhythm and pulse of Earth's life force. Also, African people should be mindful that other groups are not experiencing this liberating and peaceful, interconnected relationship with nature (Neteru). Due to their envy, and lack of the ability to sense this intimate oneness with all that exists, those with physical power and control have labeled Africans as direct descendants of great apes. Blacks should be aware of the negative connotations of repeating this educational slander or allowing others to make racist comments that Africans evolved directly from primates. Again, this statement attempts to establish a direct one-to-one correlation between Africans being a subspecies of human, who are intimate with savage demons and uncivilized animals, deserving the atrocities of chattel slavery, colonialism, and capitalism.

Moreover, dominant and controlling Abrahamic socio-religious and political indoctrination promotes that contemporary societies measure individual, family, and group success through the lens of acquiring material possessions, instead of a holistic, positive, and spiritual lifestyle in balance with nature. As mentioned previously, the destructive and warmongering religious indoctrination of domineering, oppressive groups support the false premise that African subjugation is natural and ordained by God. Any form of enslavement – mental, physical, psychic, or spiritual – violates God's intent for creating the universe and does not reflect a lifestyle of goodness and mercy to support the wellbeing of global citizens. God designed and sustains the universe so that It can have positive, loving experiences through Its creations. Most importantly, a truly spiritual lifestyle is diametrically opposed to mass, indiscriminate consumerism, which does not result in the realization of eternal peace and joy. The life purpose of those who are truly religious and seeking divinity is to acquire forms of mental and spiritual liberation, which cannot be satisfied through the Westernized version of indiscriminate deification of material possessions. Written on fiat currency, the phrase *in God we trust* is an example of how people are indoctrinated and socialized to deify and worship material possessions and its means of acquisition.

Chapter Four

Patriarchy: An Insatiable, Greco-Roman Desire to Dominate and Control Others

Historically, elitist leaders from different civilizations exchange ideas and learn from each other's successes and pitfalls at becoming gods, with the intended purpose of heavily influencing and controlling global populations, otherwise known as their slaves. A suitable description of contemporary psychic, or tax slaves are those who are mentally confined to limited empirical reality, and are unaware, or unwilling to admit to this designation. Similarly, geopolitical leadership sustains mass control by heavily manipulating people to worship men, by fighting wars and stealing territory, rich in natural resources that belongs to other nations. The shared purpose of colonialism, imperialism, and nationalism with its system of prejudicial socio-religious and economic discrimination against indigenous people and nature, was intentionally designed to enforce policies that siphons greater physical and political power, which includes material wealth for elites.

An intent of governments that follow the fascist, Western-European, and Greco-Roman paradigm is to amass material wealth for elites, primarily through military dominance, while depriving citizens of educational resources that can lead to the attainment of heightened psychic and spiritual proclivity. Evolutionary progress in terms of heightened psychic and positive spiritual proclivity are forms of advancement, which elitists have an aversion to since they are dynamic instruments of empowerment, resulting in greater mass liberation. Most important to the existential debate of mental control versus spiritual liberation is a discourse concerning a Roman religious syncretism that evolved into organized Catholicism and Christianity. In attempts to secure military and political power by pacifying territories under its control, Western-European fascism continued to take shape through socio-religious syncretism and economics to subjugate people throughout the empire.

With the collapse of the Western-Roman empire, the dark ages ensued. Before this, Emperor Constantine and the Roman Catholic church used physical force and intimidation to establish themselves as God's representative on Earth. A perverse and belligerent replica of indigenous spirituality was also implemented. From this foundation, a socio-religious structure began to dominate the lives of those within the collapsed Western empire. During the dark ages, European nobility and a patriarchal Catholic hierarchy instituted an oppressive and tyrannical version of divinity. As God's representatives on Earth, heads of state used fear tactics to maintain physical and mental control, by shaping a narrow and confined form of mass consciousness. As obstructionists misdirecting the former empire from experiencing unification with The Creator's goodness, mercy, and love, a literate Catholic hierarchy, including priests and scribes, either wrote or revised, then canonized into Abrahamic texts, specific mandates from God that justify and rationalize the warring behavior of fearmongers.

In 1431, examples of atrocities inflicted by this fearful, warmongering paradigm took the form of a Roman Catholic tribunal determining that Joan of Arc was guilty of wearing men's clothing during The Hundred Years War between England and France. Joan of Arc was burned at the stake for being a witch and heretic, but she was also perceived as a female threat to the Catholic establishment's hegemonic power structure. In approximately 1487, Pope Innocent VIII also declared, by papal bull, that witches were a real threat, due to their involvement with Satan. In 1633, Galileo Galilei was in favor of the earlier ideas of Copernicus. Still, Galileo was put on trial by the Catholic establishment for promoting a heliocentric model, or Sun-centered solar system. The heliocentric model is much older than Copernicus, however. Before Europeans used the telescope, through intuitive, shamanistic-spiritual science, African ancients, such as the Dogan people of Central Mali knew the orientation and alignment of planets and stars within the galaxy. In 16th century Europe, however, due to the expensive, extravagant, and opulent lifestyle of Pope Leo X, indulgences, or payment for the forgiveness of sin was heavily branded and peddled by the Roman Catholic power structure.

In the 17th through 19th centuries, the European enlightenment era emerged, which attempted to avoid the ignorance and corruption of Roman Catholic power brokers, promoting superstition and fear, instead of a scientific and spiritual lifestyle that reflects divinity through a balanced, close relationship with nature, along with God's goodness, mercy and love. Due to the perverted and self-serving practices embedded into European religion and spirituality, the enlightenment era attempted to distance itself from Catholic ignorance and superstition by focusing on empirical, scientific revolution and reason.

Conventional science, however, suggests that Black Africans (Homo sapien sapiens) migrated to ancient Eurasia, where they encountered and interbred with Homo floresiensis, and Neanderthals, who mated with Denisovans, otherwise known as Homo sapiens. This interbreeding resulted in the inheritance of recessive genes, which by definition are alleles not expressed in the majority of Black Africans who remained on the continent. In this case, interbreeding with Neanderthals resulted in the Caucasian phenotype. Recessive Neanderthal DNA carried by Caucasians and Asians may cause them to express deficiencies, and a less evolved ability to experience and live a positive, spiritual lifestyle compared to much older indigenous, pigmented people with close ties to nature. These inherited recessive traits also result in Europeans attempting to fill their positive-spiritual void with materialism and an empirical, atheistic version of scientific reason.

Moving into the contemporary era, a broad brush can be used to paint a picture explaining the educational philosophy that scientific inquiry must be scaffolded on an empirical foundation. To quantify the natural world, this framework heavily relies on stimulation of the five senses and data from instrumentation, which elitists can manipulate. In the current era, a powerful device employed to project, and shape mass consciousness is biased, official media analysis of edited footage that is spliced together before broadcast to form a viewing audience's contrived reality. In other words, concocted media events, such as 911, and the Kennedy assassination are staged mind-craft to create an empirical reality through mass hysteria. This has been orchestrated to keep mass populations subjugated to disinformation, while securing ruling elites' physical wealth and social status. History is replete with examples of the execution of Hegelian dialectic principles, which manipulate mass consciousness to shape perceptions of reality. Consider, also, the deceptive and misleading effects of yellow journalism and propaganda in spreading official narratives about the 1898 sinking of the USS Maine, leading up to the Spanish-American War.

In critique of more modern events compared to ancient history, a glimpse at the Western empire before its eventual 476 CE collapse, reveals that Greco-Romans established military garrisons in occupied territories primarily to quell rebellions, maintain order, and collect taxes. Greco-Roman aristocrats also intermarried and assimilated into traditional African and Eastern, hierarchical societies to solidify and embolden acceptance into indigenous societies with high spiritual culture and science. This diluted powerful-ancestral bloodlines by infusing Greco-Roman genetics into the ruling class of indigenous, priestly leadership. Seemingly, foreigners were more concerned with material wealth and had little interest in sacred, esoteric, Eastern and African-scientific knowledge, which extends beyond empirical understanding. In simple terms, the violent and treacherous lifestyle of occupying military juntas excludes them from priestly divinity, and indigenous people's spiritual power.

Using historical evidence to look back at least 5,000 years to gain insight into the liberating, spiritual and mental effects of ancient Eastern and African socio-religious and economic traditions, may conclude that initiation and rites of passage play functional roles in institutionalizing correct, moral behavior into indigenous culture. However, one intent of Abrahamic colonialism and imperialism was to sever a people from their indigenous lifestyle that celebrates God, nature, and divine ancestry. Within the twisted minds of those who instituted perpetual-chattel slavery, African people were mutated into criminality for merely being Black, and existing in a foreign land, filled with European (Judeo-Christian), along with Arab and Ottoman (Muslim) colonial enmity and bigotry. Beginning in the 7th century, Black African men who survived the tortuous trek across the Sahara Desert to become chattel slaves in the Islamic Middle East, also, endured the brutality of total castration, by having their penis and testicles amputated to make a Eunuch in charge of the harem.

Greco-Roman and Caucasian Methodology of Mass Subjugation

In America, Black people escaped the yolk of European chattel slavery by fleeing to the north, or south to Mexico. Before the 1865 end of the American civil war, White-slave catchers were law enforcement officers, who captured free Blacks along with runaway slaves, returning them to a tortured life of servitude and anguish. The larger Caucasian society supported slave catchers, as they maintained a socio-economic and political caste system that attempted to socialize and condition Blacks into a perpetual underclass, existing within a police state of White supremacists' injustice. Government institutions have also criminalized Africans, such as with the 13th Amendment of the American constitution, which as of 1865, made it lawful to re-enslave Blacks through incarceration. Throughout the diaspora, incarcerated Africans disproportionately represent a majority population. This current, dominant paradigm of neo-colonialism has also institutionalized incarceration through a police state to regulate and control mass populations, regardless of ethnicity or socio-religious affiliation. Contemporary governments modeled after the fascist, Greco-Roman state are designed to restrict and limit experiences of spiritual liberation, as with indigenous people, by implementing fear tactics and deception through Hegelian dialectic practices to maintain mass control.

The common thread in contemporary and ancient societies is that vast empires, as with the Romans, deployed occupying forces to subjugate, control, and tax mass populations. In approximately 190 CE, however, civil wars led by generals who attacked their own capital indicated that the Roman empire was on the decline. During this same period, Rome experienced a succession of incompetent emperors, who were incapable of ruling and leading the nation. Similar to modern empires, the Roman military was dispersed throughout Europe, Asia, and Northern Africa. In Rome, the seat of imperial power, military generals sought to usurp the throne, by replacing emperors known to be incompetent and ineffective. Additionally, persistent internal conflict fractured the military and weakened the empire through successive coups and civil war. Military factions fought against each other to place their desired general in power. For approximately 73 years, from 211 CE to 284 CE, 23 military emperors expropriated the throne. Of those 23 rulers, 20 were assassinated by rivals seeking sovereignty.

In addition to 73 years of civil war, the Roman Empire endured continued attacks by the Goths, Vandals, and Visigoths. These Northern tribes were seeking liberation from Rome, while acquiring warmer territories and fertile farmland. Approximately in 370 CE, another factor contributing to the decline of the Western Roman empire was the expansion of the Asian-Hunic people, who invaded Northern Europe. Invasion by the Hunnic empire placed pressure on the Goths, Vandals and Visigoths in Northern Europe, thereby causing movement southward to invade and occupy Rome in 410 CE. In approximately 284 CE, before Hunnic, Goth, Vandal, and Visigoth encroachment, Emperor Diocletian began to realize that the military was spread thin and far-reaching, making its territories vulnerable to attack by invading armies. The combination of civil war, invading foreigners, and a dispersed and weakened military, debilitated Rome's administrative ability to effectively govern its empire. Attempting to alleviate internal (civil war) and external (foreign invader) pressures, Diocletian divided the empire to make it more manageable.

The Consumption of a Lead-Based Substance Called Sapa

Historical evidence supports that before the Common Era (CE), Asiatic or Persians (Hittites and possibly Hyksos), as well as Greek occupying forces, and Roman invaders emulated, and attempted to assimilate into ancient Egyptian (Kemetic) high civilization and spiritual culture. Comparatively speaking, contemporary Western civilization, with its origin in ancient Greco-Roman society, cannot replicate many spiritual, megalithic, artistic, and cultural accomplishments of Kemet and Africa. Excessively focusing on physical and empirical reality to gain material possessions, Greco-Romans fail to acknowledge the value of practices that stimulate psychic centers to develop cultures grounded in enhanced intuition and spiritual science. Not being synchronized with nature, and not functioning at higher levels of consciousness, ancient Greco-Romans invented and consumed a toxic, lead (Pb) derived sweetener, sapa. Contemporary attempts to recreate sapa results in a lethal, lead-based liquid, not meant for consumption. Perhaps the average aristocrat, who voluntarily drank their own *Kool-Aid* by consumed large quantities of sapa tainted wine, explains their abhorrent behaviors, culminating in civil wars and assassination.

Consuming lead-tainted sapa could have added to the nobility's mental derangement, thereby exacerbating delusions of grandeur, resulting in militaristic behaviors that enforced demented power relationships, where Roman emperors had to be venerated as gods. As such, human subjects or citizens who can be controlled by their emotions, and lower-animal nature or spirit, have been conditioned to pay taxes as forms of tribute to support a system, or god that did not, and does not serve their best interest. Elitist emperors and geopolitical leaders are deemed divine gods, while everyone else, tax-slaves, citizens, and subjects are emotional humans controlled by a system of corrupt, insensitive overlords. The same as in the modern era, the Roman credo was *bread and circuses* – to ensure that no real systemic change ever takes place, keep the masses (citizen and slave populations) distracted, occupied, entertained, enamored and delusional. In the past, entertainment took place in coliseums. Today it takes place in sport stadiums and the political arena.

Irrespective of sapa consumption, by 293 CE, Diocletian successfully restructured the Roman government by establishing the tetrarchy: A system of rule involving four men who shared physical power over the massive Roman empire. Ruled by two separate men: an Augustus and a Caesar. The Latin speaking, Western empire comprised Spain, France, England, Italy, and parts of Germany. The Greek speaking, Eastern empire had its own Augustus and Caesar, and this territory's capital later became Constantinople (modern-day Turkey), which ruled the Byzantine region. Dividing territory did not solve the issues. To a major extent, it may have exacerbated the problem by creating the need to fortify massive territories.

As stated previously: Elitist geopolitical leadership or emperors learn from the success and pitfalls of other civilizations. Rarely is it discussed that the Roman slave population grew to capacity. Not being Roman citizens, enslaved populations also were not a source of tax revenue, which resulted in loss of income for national coffers. With the empire divided into Western and Eastern territories, more fortifications were needed to protect separate tributaries that fed a growing empire – this required funding through increased taxation of Roman citizens.

Compared to modern governments that acquire revenue from most of its population: legal immigrants or green-card holders, as well as naturalized and native-born citizens, the tax base of the Western and Eastern empires were severely limited due to an extensive, untaxed slave population. Roman citizens were burdened with higher taxes, and more coins were minted to fund military fortifications, which led to inflation and higher prices. Generally, these factors resulted in a population that was increasingly dissatisfied with its empire or burgeoning form of government. Some previously mentioned, along with new and different influences also contributed to the collapse of the Western Roman Empire: Persistent encroachment and the threat of invasion by Northern Goths and Vandals, fiscal and financial problems in Rome, as well as citizens who were inclined to understand that they were subservient to an elitist, central administration that was self-serving and dysfunctional.

Throughout history, Roman emperors have successfully preserved their legacy by infusing themselves into a type of pagan-religious syncretism, where they are depicted in spiritual iconography to form shared power alliances with a burgeoning Christian church. As time progressed, for a great number of people, however, irreconcilable church differences exist. For example, the conflict between the seemingly idolatrous traditions of Roman Catholicism, compared to that of Christian Protestants, who claim to be pure and pious, due to forms of veneration that lack religious iconography and idol worship.

To clarify, in 325 CE, when Christianity became an organized religion, a pagan, or idol worshipper was anyone who was not a Catholic adherent to the Nicene Creed. Seemingly, for Catholics (Roman, English, and Orthodox): iconography, artwork, and even graven images are acceptable forms of religiosity, if it depicts the life, death, and resurrection of the Savior, and saints associated with these events. Whether due to ignorance, or an unwillingness to admit to the oneness, or unifying qualities of spiritual science, these saints are supposed to represent the same positive energies personified through initiates, African ancestors, and forces of nature. For elitists, The Supreme Being's unifying qualities are counterproductive to the divide and conquer tactics of aristocrats, who maintain mass control through subjugation.

Modern fascist states and governments follow the same hypocritical and biased socio-religious practices that resulted in Greco-Roman dominance to create mass-control systems through historical military and political maneuvers. Since Westerners proudly trace their military and civil heritage to fascist, Greco-Roman rule, it would be disingenuous to say that democratic forms of government cannot be fascist in nature and origin. Similarly, contemporary governments also tend to practice forms of corporate fascism.

In contrast, to develop and maintain high spiritual culture, ancient societies were centered around studying the flow of subtle, balanced energies within nature that manifests as peace and harmony in all that exists. Through intuitive, spiritual science, the ancients also studied the cyclic movement of constellations and planets to create calendars predicting transitions to a new era, with complementary shifts in consciousness levels. Due to a lack of respect for indigenous lifestyles that maintain connections to nature, and their deliberate inability to practice and cultivate positive-spiritual science, inquiries should be made into specific Popes and Bishops who were corrupt and perverted, but still beatified into Catholic sainthood.

A Nationalistic Tradition of Writing Texts that Celebrates War and Conquest

Other than Emperor Diocletian of 293 CE, who successfully divided the empire into a tetrarchy, Flavius Constantine is one of Rome's most renowned rulers. It is estimated that in 275 CE, he was born into an aristocratic bloodline and heritage. Before formation of the tetrarchy, however, Constantine's father was a military commander and Caesar of the Western region. Instead of referring to him as exclusively Constantine, the title or name, Flavius, is appended. During his early years, Flavius Constantine lived in the imperial court, eventually serving as a high-ranking staff officer to Diocletian, himself.

His name, Flavius, may stem from the Piso Flavian dynasty, a Roman imperial bloodline that ruled the empire beginning in 69 CE, also known as the Year of the Four Emperors. By ending the civil war of 69 CE, the Piso Flavians gained control for a 27-year period, from 69 CE to 96 CE. At that time, most people throughout the empire were illiterate, however. The Piso Flavians were members of a literate minority and ruling elite, who enforced policies, and compiled socio-religious text intended to indoctrinate and subjugate the empire. To support, rationalize, and justify negative emotionalism that is fomented by humankind, but portrayed as God's work and desire, written into socio-religious text and indoctrination is war, murder, theft, and other atrocities.

Often, there is no clear and definitive understanding of the phrase: *God's chosen people,* who perpetrate the previously mentioned atrocities. However, the involvement and interference of *God's chosen people*, such as the Piso Flavians, shapes another dichotomy. This is one where an all merciful and loving God: The Supreme Being and Creator of all things, seemingly, becomes in favor of war, murder, theft, and all other atrocities. Driven by greed and the acquisition of material possessions, other than the Piso Flavians, the Hebrew historian and scholar, Flavius Josephus was another literate elitist, who was involved in this conflicted process of rationalizing destructive, murderous behavior.

Clearly, throughout history there has been a hierarchical tradition where nobility, priests, and military leadership comprised a literate aristocracy. Holding aristocratic membership, the Piso Flavians and others have intervened to shape Abrahamic scriptures and spiritual texts to make it appear that God, The Creator of all things, is a manipulative and imperialistic nationalist, who is jealous, hateful, and favors one group over another. According to their perverse understanding of The Creator Being, ruling elites have put in place and established a literary construct, where God's favored people are also negative, murderous, and militaristic.

Undeniably, history is written by the victor or conqueror. *God's chosen* or favored people also write history – their story from the perspective of a militaristic, domineering group lacking in knowledge of The Creator and positive spirituality. They are also inspired to write cryptic, scriptural text which borrows from much older writings, oral traditions, and philosophies of native, indigenous people. These texts have become cryptic because the Ptolemaic, Piso Flavians, and others like them have interwoven their chaotic emotional, and murderous behavior into literature, forming belief systems that developed into a popularized mindset, and philosophical thought that conveys a brand of negative spirituality.

Due to detachment from positive-spiritual ancestry, and a lack of understanding of divine providence, modern humans (Homo sapien sapiens) often choose to engage in negative behavior that originates from the primal brain stem, or lower animal nature. In this case, behavior is the same as that of a selfish reptile, who is not concerned with this planet, or its own offspring, siblings, and species. Similarly, Piso Flavian leadership and fascism's contemporary embodiment are incarnated through militaristic fearmongers and geopolitical policies. Under the guise of national security, ritualized cannibalism to sacrifice body and blood is fulfilled through Piso Flavian incarnates, committing acts of war and terror. These groups of elitists also attempt to make it appear that their crimes against humanity are a supreme and natural order, so they blame God for their original sin, or reptile-like behavior and actions.

Bear in mind that Constantine and areas under Roman control did not abandon paganism. Rather, Catholicism and paganism coexist within a syncretic system, challenging people to distinguish between the two. On October 8th, 312 CE, Constantine won the battle at the Milvian Bridge, which crosses the Tiber River. One of the most well-known and memorable official narratives concerning Constantine's conquest of the

Western sector is as follows: *At the Tiber River in 312 CE, he had a vision during travels to battle Maxentius, his most powerful rival in Italy.*

Chapter Five

To Consolidate Power and to be Venerated as a God, Emperor Constantine Organizes a New Socio-religious Syncretism

Simcha Jacobovici is a documentary filmmaker who televised the series, *Decoding the Ancients: Selling Christianity* on the History Channel. Based on his extensive research of primary-source evidence and interviews with professional scholars and experts, Mr. Jacobovici says that: "Christianity, as it currently exists, is a religion created by Flavius Constantine." One of his sources of primary evidence is The Arch of Constantine. To tell his narrative in sculpture, commemorating the victory over Maxentius at the Milvian Bridge, Constantine commissioned construction of the nine-story arch in the center of Rome, shortly after 312 CE. In this episode, Mr. Jocobovici's guest is Professor Elizabeth Marlowe of Colgate University, NY. Together, they investigate The Arch of Constantine to answer critical questions confronting traditional-Christian narratives that evolved into unsubstantiated history.

Approximately 1,200 years after the battle at the Milvian Bridge, in 1520 CE, Pope Julius II commissioned artist Raphael to paint Vatican walls, commemorating Constantine's vision of Christ and consequential conversion to Christianity. Following the tradition of incorrect belief, Raphael's art became a history that depicts Constantine's soldiers as vastly outnumbered, but they still brandished banners and shields painted with the cross of Christ. The traditional Christian narrative precedes Raphael's fresco through history acclaiming Constantine's vision and dream of Christ, which results in denouncing ancestral pagan traditions in favor of new-found beliefs. Primary source evidence from Constantine's arch tells a different story, however.

According to Professor Marlowe, while examining sculpted depictions of the battle on The Arch of Constantine, there is no evidence of his conversion to Christianity. There is no cross on the military standard carried by the soldier standing behind Constantine in this artwork, and none is sculpted into shields held by other soldiers. Professor Marlowe, and documentary film-maker Mr. Jacobovici confirm: "When the primary source is looked at, there is no evidence of Constantine's vision or conversion to Christianity."

On the entire Arch, there is no Christian iconography whatsoever. Encircling the structure are eight-huge statues of Magi-looking figures, wearing hats referred to as a Phrygian cap. As the narrator of the documentary suggests, these caps are symbolic of non-Christian wise men or Eastern and African initiates into intuitive spiritual systems of knowledge. Here is a socio-religious syncretism, or blending of religious beliefs between Mithraism and Christianity, since the three-wise men, or Magi are also depicted wearing the Phrygian cap in the nativity scene at Saint Apollinaire Nuovo, one of the oldest Christian churches in Italy. Mithraism predates Christianity. This cap's adornment seems to signify clarity of thought and vision to pierce higher reality levels while participating in initiation to become god, Mithras. As stated previously, monotheistic Christianity may have become the Roman national religion, but clearly, paganism is accepted and infiltrates global traditions and customs throughout Christendom and Abrahamic systems of belief.

Consciousness-elevating ceremonies, with origins in paganism, may have helped Constantine with understanding the importance of initiation to cultivate virtues to transcend selfishness and corrupt, political self-dealing. Through art, Constantine may have been promoting initiation systems that cultivate specific virtues before holding esteemed public office that requires service to others. Quite possibly, the Phrygian cap, and most definitely the Ozo, signifies the relevance and importance of virtuous initiation. The Phrygian cap's symbology and history predate its modern European interpretation, indicating prominence and a desire for freedom and liberty. In Nigeria's much older socio-historical and cultural traditions, the Igbo people wear a similar hat referred to as the Ozo. Igbos, who have risen in stature through rites of passage and initiation, wear the hat, similar to the Magi of the nativity scene, and on the Arch of Constantine.

Further on in the documentary, Mr. Jocobovici interviews Professor Raymond Van Dam of the University of Michigan. He talks about church father and Bishop, Eusebius Pamphilus,

Constantine's biographer and close confidant. Here, again, primary-source evidence supports that Constantine did not have a vision of Christ before battling Maxentius at the Milvian Bridge. Neither did Constantine denounce his ancestral-pagan traditions. In Pamphilus' first draft of the battle, there is no record of Constantine's vision mentioned in the primary-source text, *Imperatoris Constantini Liber Primus.* Similarly, Kerrie L. French says, in the PDF article *Constantine's Creation of Jesus Christ*:

> It appears that in 325 CE, a new god was conceived within the black and white marble halls of Roman Catholicism. Constantine's intention at Nicaea was to create an entirely new god for his empire who would unite [and pacify] all [territories and] religious factions under one deity.

Constantine's story, where he saw the cross of Christ superimposed on the Sun with the words, in hoc signo vinces: *In this sign, you shall conquer,* is considered historical. Truth be told, it is challenging to read while staring into the Sun. He did not have specially made sunglasses that allowed him to read the specific phrase: hoc signo vinces. As it was then and is still true today, Christ is a spiritual leader, who did not promote and support war, murder, human slaughter, or conquest. Neither did he require monetary tribute for spiritual services rendered. However, geopolitical leader, Constantine, won the battle at the Tiber River in 312 CE. While slaughtering Maxentius' troops, many of Constantine's soldiers died as well. As a living initiate into the pantheon of gods or the Roman Imperial Cult, the epiphany that Constantine received at the Tiber River, may have been strategies for unifying territories under one theocratic state, within this polytheistic religion of which he is the absolute and supreme ruler.

The Vision of the Cross: Edits to Constantine's Official Biography

To unify Roman territories under the banner of a burgeoning belief system, Constantine's primary accomplice and confidant Eusebius Pamphilus, Christian Bishop, Presbyter, and church father was an influential operative, who helped Constantine to become supreme ruler of the military, religious, and geopolitical machine. Based on Pamphilus' writing in the *Imperatoris Constantini Liber Primus,* 13-years after the battle at the Milvian Bridge, in 325 CE, he was persuaded to edit the biography to include a vision: the dream of Christ. Professor Van Dam sources the firsthand account as he says that Constantine informed Pamphilus, at the Council of Nicaea, that the narrative must proceed as follows: *First, the vision of a cross in the sky at noon. Secondly, his dream, where Jesus Christ, himself, appears to explain the vision.* At that moment of hearing this prophetic narrative, Pamphilus envisions the emperor as the embodiment of the second coming of Jesus. In this update or edit of the biography, Constantine appears to be a prophet, spiritual leader, and incarnation of Christ, who codifies newly formed Christian beliefs.

The spiritual power of The Supreme Being does not discriminate. However, the purpose of unifying and pacifying Roman-held territories under one supreme ruler and religion was, and still is the goal of Roman Catholicism, which means universal. Through spiritual and metaphysical means, accessing an unlimited universe to reveal the secret or hidden qualities of an omnipresent, omnipotent, and omniscient God provides a corrupt geopolitical machine with increased power to deceive others. In simple terms, modern humans (Homo sapien sapiens) are transitioning through an evolutionary period, where the will and the right to choose is critical and paramount. Choosing to access spiritual power to establish a relationship of beneficent reciprocity between God and humankind brings balanced and harmonious living to the entire species and planet.

Then, again, people who practice negative emotionalism: Greed, selfishness, and political self-dealing can also access this power. In this case, however, power results in self-destruction and physical and emotional harm to others. From its inception, the goal of an elitists' Roman Catholic hierarchy has been the accumulation of material possessions through physical, metaphysical, or spiritual means. The critical point of contention questions a corrupt, individual lifestyle and a perverted and immoral group dynamic.

Experiences on this Earthly, physical plane of existence teach that anywhere elitists appear, it is as gods with the power to enslave others. However, their actions and behavior are negative, counterintuitive, and disrespectful of God, The Creator of all things. As mentioned previously, the purpose of specific educational theories and practices, such as strict evolution is to limit and confine humankind to empirical and physical levels of consciousness. Due to limited psychic evolution and experiences of insight into spiritual reality, the conditioned and programmed uninitiated masses accept the biased and incorrect supposition that Earth is the only place in an infinite universe where life exists.

Standardized Western education also insists that physical life-forms are the only types that exist, and interdimensional, spirit beings are based in superstition, and are therefore irrelevant or nonexistent. From a defensive posture, and to insulate their domain from humankind, which confines itself to physical reality and lower consciousness levels: overwhelmingly positive and loving, more highly evolved forms of spiritual and interdimensional life, will not commune with those who are restricted to fearful, warmongering thoughts, emotions, and actions. Here is a precise and definitive understanding of divinity: More highly evolved spiritual, symbiotic beings will not take up residence, or reside in a host-vehicle that is defiled and consumed with self-serving materialism.

The 325 CE Council of Nicaea

As mentioned previously, nine years after Flavius Constantine's birth, in 284 CE, Emperor Diocletian divided the empire into a tetrarchy, with four quadrants ruled by two Augustus and two minor Caesars. To stabilize the empire, Diocletian attempted to deter ongoing chaos, anarchy, and civil war caused by military generals usurping the throne through murder and treason. Roman emperors were so-called polytheists, who worshipped a pantheon of gods and coerced most occupants of their territories into venerating the established order of leadership, thought to be demigods. Heavily persuading or forcing others to practice the emperor's national religion is a form of manipulation to pacify Rome's occupants and territories. In this theocratic state, the emperor is a living god and an initiate into the pantheon of gods. It would be sacrilege to rebel against the emperor, who is a god incarnate. Acts of terror, along with socio-religious indoctrination and socialization are deterrents that reduce mob, or mass violence against the state, due to fear of god's divine retribution. Similarly, taxes are paid to god as a form of tribute.

Like previous military leaders and emperors, Constantine wanted to be worshipped, deified, and made into a living god. Unlike his predecessors, however, he successfully devised methods to bolster church Bishops' assistance. By unifying a military, socio-religious, and geopolitical machine, Constantine and ecumenical leadership gained greater wealth, power, and control over their subjects. Before 325 CE and the council of Nicaea, socio-religious text already existed that narrated the life and events of Yeshua (Savior), Joshua, Yesus, or Jesus. As Ms. French implies, a caucus in Nicaea agreed on a shared pronunciation, along with the positive-spiritual attributes of this revisited and revised Roman savior. Also, to be decided were meditative scripts, scripture, or socio-religious text to be included in this new compilation of Biblical canon. A Catholic oath or pledge, known as the Nicaean Creed, is an underpinning of Christianity that also emerged from the council of 325 CE.

In her writing, Ms. French, interprets the *Historia Ecclesiastica* (church history) from the 5th-century historian, Socrates Scholasticus of Constantinople, who documented ecumenical events from 305 CE to 439 CE. This is a 134-year period in which Socrates Scholasticus continued to write about Catholic, or organized church history, where Eusebius Pamphilus (Constantine's biographer) ended his narration. Relative to the discussion of historical, geopolitical tactics of using empirical and spiritual, or psychic means to control, and confine humankind to physical reality, the PDF article by Ms. French is most relevant. She writes about the Presbyters or Bishops' council, who were delegates from Roman held territories at the Council of Nicaea.

Based on their specific area of origin, Presbyters were thought to be holy, scholarly men with significant influence on their followers. Constantine's motive and those of the Presbyters, such as Eusebius Pamphilus, should be brought into question, however. Is it that they wanted to evaluate and compile doctrine to synthesize texts that would teach methods for acquiring mental liberation? In contrast, is it to establish hegemonic relationships that exclude citizens, subjects, and laypeople from higher levels of divinity, based on aristocratic teaching and sermons promoting elites as the embodiment, and incarnation of the only begotten son of God? Part of this elitists belief system is a tradition where clergymen who sermonize, proselytize, and message the only begotten son of God are its embodiment and incarnate, as well. Laypeople begin to falsely accept this tradition of psycho-spiritual antics as being correct and truthful. This results in further assumptions that the socio-religious system itself and its messengers are holy, spiritually enlightened, and deserving of tithes or tribute.

This overarching, hegemonic relationship of entanglement ties the state to clergymen and laypeople so that tribute, taxes, and tithes are willingly paid or coerced through paycheck deductions. These relationships and interactions appear deployed to support elitists' socio-religious systems and government control. Specific to the doctrine of fear and eternal damnation, these relationships are linked to forms of psychological, or psychic ransom, spiritual degradation, and evolutionary sabotage.

In 325 CE, Flavius Constantine brought together Presbyters, or Christian Bishops, as he convened the council of Nicaea held in the Eastern sector, or modern-day Turkey. Constantine was not, but neither were the Presbyters spiritual leaders with the intended purpose of teaching, or even offering methodologies to attain mass-mental liberation, and physical healing. Unlike Constantine, however, the Presbyters were trained in analysis and compilation of religious doctrine, and Ms. French writes the following: "At the council of Nicaea, Presbyters were asked to debate and decide who their god would be. Delegates argued among themselves, expressing personal motives for the inclusion of particular writings that promoted the finer traits of their special deity." This seems similar to modern political conventions, where party delegates vote and choose the candidate favored by their region or constituency.

During Constantine's reign, people may have also wanted political representation through Presbyters and their regional god being ever-present in the Roman pantheon. Similar to modern politicians and geopolitical leadership, Presbyters are self-serving. They lobbied to include their specific regional doctrine concerning the subtle, more acceptable traits or qualities of certain deities, and affiliated socio-religious teachings into Constantine's new holy book. For the Presbyters, among their many other privileges, the power to lobby or petition Emperor Constantine brought with it prestigious rewards of honor, wealth, and socio-political status.

In the modern era, we can compare the candidate's political speeches to particular writings or doctrines that promote special deities' finer traits at the Council of Nicaea. Recent speeches and debates are supposed to provide greater insight into the candidate's ideological perspective and policies for the region, nation, or people, if elected to political office. Seemingly, constituents want to understand the mindset or mental prowess of their candidate of choice. They also want a form of allusive assurance that their candidate has shared goals and objectives as the region, nation, and people. To clarify, taxpayers want to know that their candidate is working to improve their quality of life instead of fulfilling an implicit elitists' agenda, which is often the case.

Chapter Six

The Veneration of Mithras

Concerning the Council of Nicaea convened in 325 CE, which was both an ecumenical and political convention, Ms. French writes the following:

> Throughout the meeting, howling factions immersed in heated debates, tabled the names of 53 gods. At the end of that time, Constantine returned to the gathering to discover that the Presbyters had not agreed on a new deity, but had balloted down to a shortlist of five prospects: Caesar, Crishna [Krishna], Mithra, Horus, and Zeus [Roman Jupiter].

In general, Western-male patriarchy's physical dominance may be due to their overemphasis on limited analytical, or segregative thinking that isolates the parts, or components of the whole. Assume then that this collective, divisive, and myopic mindset also dominated the all-male cohort of the Nicaean council, who identified with, and celebrated Greco-Roman war and conquest. This analytical, left-brain, male-dominated thinking is excluded, or restricted from a more holistic worldview. Seemingly, segregative thinking challenges Westerners and the Abrahamic tradition to conceptualize and experience an all-encompassing and inclusive supreme Creator Being. They also lack experience of two fundamental principles: God is love, and Its consciousness exists in all things.

The subtle influence of xenophobic, Abrahamic traditions, beliefs, and bias has infiltrated mainstream, corporate media to possibly cause internal conflict for some people. For the uninitiated masses, often words from the altar of Abrahamic clergy, and imagery through entertainment media weave together an illusional reality of communing with the natural world, as sorts of shamanic, ritualized nature worship to consort with the devil through demon possession. This bias results in a reluctance to entertain thoughts, cultivate emotions, and carry out actions linked to a positive, indigenous-spiritual lifestyle that emulates God's existence, as experienced through the balance and harmony within nature.

In opposition to Abrahamic doctrine, here is a straightforward yet somewhat scientific rendition and understanding of creation. In the beginning, approximately 13.9 billion-years-ago, a singularity of pure consciousness existed. By definition, a singularity is pure and all of one thing: This consciousness was aware and knew that it was alone. God willed to differentiate and create infinite manifestations of Itself by becoming heavy and dense, then exploding, which resulted in the Big Bang and a limitless, ever-expanding universe. Its consciousness or awareness exists in all things, animate and inanimate, since everything originates from this Creator Being. From that explosion or Big Bang emanates God's consciousness and awareness, which are the institutional, structural framework of particles foundational to scientific laws and principles, maintaining a balanced, harmonious, and ordered universe. God creates so that It can have positive, loving experiences through Its creations, in which consciousness resides.

Simultaneously emanating from this explosion, or Big Bang is spiraling energy (light, sound, and electromagnetic radiation), as well as spirit, that merges to form particles, or physical matter, from which all things come into existence. In some traditions, a symbolic, comic egg describes the shape of the universe. Life emerges from an egg, similar to organisms evolving on planets within an ever-expanding universe. Ancient, pigmented people experience through ritualized prayer, and meditation that all things contain energy or spirit that exists at different states, or levels of density. To better understand that the underlying subtle, and often imperceptible flow of energy, or spirit, is the force that can be influenced by consciousness to shape physical matter, a discussion of similarities between *Mithra, Krishna,* and Heru or *Horus* is relevant. As an exact science, Eastern and ancient African people understand and study this universal flow of energy, or spirit, which can be influenced by conscious awareness.

In contrast, today, due to socio-religious indoctrination, and conventional academia, the study of universal Qi, Kundalini, Ra, Vril, or spirit is viewed and labeled as superstition and Voodoo. To specific groups of ancient-pigmented people, the study of spirituality, or subtle, flowing biochemical and universal bioelectric and electromagnetic energies is an exact science. Yet, conventional academia is probably unwilling to agree with spiritual science. However, experimentation has proven that matter and energy are neither created nor destroyed but converts to something different. This spiritual, or conventional and empirical scientific law is referred to as the conservation of consciousness, energy, and matter. The creationist who is mindful enough to take an eclectic approach might say that everything is recycled, and goes back to Source, or The Creator of the Big Bang, which is the same as The Creator of all things.

These primal and natural forces or energies from creation exist today and continue to shape and manipulate physical matter. Everything, especially spiritual, or electromagnetic and bioelectric energy, converts, shifts, or recycles into different forms to reside in physical matter, such as biological organisms. This spirit or energy component of animate objects also returns to Source, the inner planes, or God. This energy component or spirit is then reborn, or incarnated into different physical vehicles, or flesh and blood bodies. For example, *Mithra, Krishna,* and Heru or *Horus* personality types are angelic energies with different qualities of expression, depending on the physical host-vehicle. Most crucial for refined and proper expression of angelic qualities is the hosts' lifestyle and their ability to purify, stimulate, awaken, and arouse certain psychic centers or chakras. Devotees study the positive qualities of specific devas, deities, angels, Neteru, Orishas, saints, or ancestors. They also meditate using mantras, or hekau to stimulate psychic centers, while cultivating angelic energies to find answers to real-world concerns. The previous descriptions may explain what it means to be an avatar, or to carry an ancestor, or Loa (Lwa).

Mithraism: A Precursor to Syncretic Roman Catholicism and Organized Christianity

About the energies of god Mithra, or the mystery religion, Mithraism, a quote from the Roman philosopher Seneca is most relevant:

> Someday the secrets of nature shall be disclosed to you, the haze will be lifted from your eyes, and the bright light will stream in upon you from all sides. Picture to yourself how great is the glow when all the stars mingle their fires; no shadow will disturb the clear sky ...

The Roman philosopher, Seneca, lived for approximately 69 years, and he died in 65 CE. Seneca borrowed and learned from much older traditions and philosophers. For example, Mithras is the Roman name for the Indo-Iranian god Mitra, and it is by that name that the Persians knew him. Before the god Mitra became the Roman Mithras, it was one of the minor gods under Ahura-Mazda in the Zoroastrian pantheon, from 1,500 BCE, which predates the philosophies of Seneca. In the Zoroastrian pantheon, Mitra is also one of the yazatas, or minor gods who presides over light, which mediates between heaven and Earth. Mitra is also mentioned in the Vedas, and other ancient Hindu traditions, which may predate the Zoroastrian pantheon, from 1,500 BCE.

The secrets of nature, which Seneca speaks about, are the previously referenced primal spiritual or energetic forces from creation. He is alluding to traditional psychic and metaphysical rituals and practices, such as prayer, meditation, yoga, and Qi Gong, which connect to this underlying, primal flow of energy that can be manipulated to shape physical occurrences. In so doing, *the haze*, or veil of deception will be *lifted from your eyes*, as Seneca says. The bright light signifies aspects of enlightenment or spiritual liberation, clarity, and clairvoyance to gaze into the shadows, to see past elitists' empirical deception. This is achieved through psychic rituals and practices to understand that everything is interconnected and interrelated through God's consciousness, which is the order that controls or modifies all things in existence. Again, God's consciousness is universal, and by understanding the creation process, a pure life that reflects Its image and likeness can be lived, so that humankind can transition to gods on Earth, who have earned their rightful place in the heavens and in the universe.

Other than Zoroastrianism and Mithraism, the Abrahamic, socio-religious tradition says that angels and archangels were created before modern humans (Homo sapien sapiens). This clarifying statement agrees with ancient, non-Western traditions that accept and experience the existence of angelic beings that are older, and therefore, more spiritually evolved forms of life. In simple terms, angelic beings have been in existence for longer periods, and have transitioned or evolved to higher consciousness levels and spiritual awareness. It is also stated that these higher beings do not have the right to choose, but are in continual service to God, and abide by Its natural, harmonious laws. In so doing, higher forms of life gain benefit, relative to their realm of existence and the universe at large.

Saying that angelic beings do not have the freedom to choose implies that their will is inactive. They therefore cannot execute that which is contrary to divine law as reflected through

God's spirit and consciousness dwelling in all things and nature. Higher beings referred to as angels, and archangels do have the will, and freedom to choose. However, they make the ultimate difference by influencing occurrences, and communing with people in this fourth-dimensional reality, who choose to align their thoughts, emotions, and actions to that which is under God's divine law. These behaviors are to the benefit of the entire universe.

About the fallen angel, who chooses to disobey the divine laws of God and nature, clearly, this speaks of the current, pervasive state of spiritual stagnation in humankind. This is one where the favored choice is to cultivate negative emotions of fear and jealousy against older, more spiritually evolved forms of pigmented people, who have close ties to nature. The call challenges modern humans to spiritually evolve and resist the impulse to adhere to their own internal demons: fear, anger, jealousy, etc.

Regarding the history of Western-spiritual understanding, or lack thereof, Simcha Jacobovici describes Mithraism in the documentary film *"Decoding the Ancients: Selling Christianity"*. Mr. Jacobovici interviews Professor John F. Shean of LaGuardia Community College, NY, who discusses primary-source evidence buried below one of the world's first Roman Catholic or Christian churches, Santa Prisca, in Rome. Under the baseboards and flooring of this church, one of the largest Mithraeums is found.

It appears that Christians build churches on top of older Mithraic, and other temples that are aligned to intersecting ley lines to amplify human spiritual energy by combining it with Earth's electromagnetic field. Using forms of ancient-divination science, they detected ley lines or Earth's flowing electromagnetic field, which intersect to rise with scalar, focused power. Those who ritualized in ancient temples, and worship in contemporary churches, commingle and magnify their devotional energies with that of Earth's living electromagnetic flow to reach, communicate, and share spiritual power with angelic beings, residing in the heavens and on other worlds. This is an example of ancient, spiritual technology that uses megaliths, and other structures to allow humankind to commune with ancestors, as well as interdimensional and otherworldly beings.

Ancient temples, or churches, were communication devices where modern humans (Homo sapien sapiens) performed rituals to transition to higher levels of spiritual evolution. With limited success at communication, in the contemporary era, empirical science uses radio telescope technology, such as SETI (Search for Extraterrestrial Intelligence). Success is limited compared to the magnificent accomplishments of ancient, megalithic architecture, and high-spiritual culture that celebrates African divine ancestry.

As evidence of forms of devolution and declining cultivation of intuitive talents tied to spiritual science, most modern congregation members are deterred from, and detest divination traditions and methodologies. The message from the pulpit of those professing specific Abrahamic traditions is that divination, equivalent to yoga and meditation, opens portals to hell, allowing demonic possession of diviners and those in attendance. Conversely, there is real-world, life-science research, where divination oracles, such as Ifa, I Ching, the Metu Neter, and the Holy Bible can be used to access two-way communication with God, for problem solving. However,

Western tradition seems to categorize oracle systems, including the Holy Bible as prophetic, fortune telling devices, which is often not the case. The mere act of using a specific type of divination system, does not automatically activate a suspicious omen of fortitude, or dilemma.

Spiritual power is not in the device, or particular oracle system, but is in the practitioner's receptivity to change behavior to actualize the positive message, or outcome from the reading. Ancient-knowledge system practitioners who are detached from their ego, intellect, and lower, negative-emotional nature often partake in a lifestyle of meditation, and use oracle readings to access direct, two-way communication with God. Emotional and intellectual detachment, and humility are prerequisites to implement messages from oracle systems practiced in real-life, and real-world situations. By filtering the ego, with its negative thoughts, emotions, and actions, the practitioner gains access to a more pure and divine form of reality, along with greater spiritual influence and power. A different form of divination using dowsing technology detects underground water sources. A practice similar to dowsing rod usage may have been applied to detect Earth's magnetic field, with intersecting ley lines.

In Simcha Jacobovici's documentary film, Professor Shean also proceeds to mention that Roman generals and officers congregated in a sort of military-elitists' cult in Mithraic grotto-like temples, constructed prior to, but today found underneath certain Christian churches. During this era, in Rome, initiation into the Mithraic mystery cult may have preceded ascension through the ranks of military succession. Enlisted men, common-Roman citizens, and most certainly slaves were denied entry. The Mithraeum underneath Santa Prisca church has a recreation of the grotto-like temple, seemingly chiseled into solid rock depicting the primal cave where Mithras commits the sacrifice of the bull. On occasion, Mithras wears the Phrygian cap. Often clothed in Roman-military regalia, Mithra's arm and hand literally grabs the bull by a horn. The other hand brandishes a knife used to shed blood by stabbing the sacrificial bull in the torso.

Chapter Seven

Ritualized Blood Sacrifice: To Control Others Through Fear

According to Professor Shean, this bloodletting motif is ". . . a core advance in Mithraism." In this semi-subterranean temple, only one small window illuminates the centerpiece of Mithras, the son of the Sun. Professor Shean further explains the symbolism in this grotto by saying: "Through shedding blood of the sacrificial bull, the universe is created anew." To his devotees, Mithras is perceived as a key creator god, who makes possible the regeneration of life. Jacobovici also comments by saying: "The primordial rock, onto which the blood of the sacrificial bull is shed is similar to a cocoon out of which the universe is born anew."

Generally, inscriptions are lacking in most pagan Mithraeums. However, under the Christian Santa Prisca church, etched graffiti is found in close proximity to the central bloodletting motif, which translates from Latin to read the following: *Thou hast saved us by shedding the eternal blood.* Jacobovici says that "This central bloodletting is seen as an act of salvation."

Professor Shean concurs by explaining that bloodletting is a key event in the cosmic nature of Mithraic belief. The documentary filmmaker, and the scholar, Professor Shean, both say, "The Mithraic sacred meal of sharing bread and wine, symbolizing the sacrificial body and blood of a bull, may have evolved and transitioned into forms of communion, or the Holy Eucharist." Similarly, the credo of Mithraism was: *Those who partake in this feast will live forever.*

What is clear is that violence and the spilling of blood, whether animal or human, was the Greco-Roman path to consolidating power within its Western and Eastern empires, while dominating North Africa, and Kemet (ancient Egypt). Rooted in the narrative of Mithraism is the iconographic or literal spilling of blood, as with the sacrifice of the bull. Historically, through art and sculpture, the god, Ausar, was often phenotypically depicted with Black, African features. Literally, through war and invasion, Black, Africans who venerated and lived as an Ausar were slaughtered by Persians and Greco-Romans, who through syncretism created their Caucasian god, Osiris. Genocidal war and destruction were to decimate Black, Africans and Ausar so that syncretism could cause the Caucasian, Osiris to exist. This is a form of usurpation of African spirituality through violence. Professor Shean, an expert in Mithraic symbology says that ". . . in the bloodletting motif, lifeforce is spilled onto a primordial mound of Earth, causing the rebirth of the universe, represented by the emergence of Osiris, a Greco-Roman god with a lock of hair on its forehead."

Mithraic iconography implies that Greco-Romans are the resurrected Caucasian god, Osiris. The prehistoric god, Ausar, may have died as an African, but more modern history suggests that he resurrected as a Greco-Roman Mithras, Osiris, and Christlike savior. Now, Africans should resurrect themselves in the image and likeness of their ancient priestly ancestors and fore parents.

The Greco-Roman has sought to distract humankind from the deeply rooted aspiration to cultivate its divine nature to achieve aspects of spiritual liberation and clairvoyance. Throughout the ages, the Greco-Roman has devised and instituted socio-economic and political systems that distract humankind from its divinity, resulting in the worship of men, material possessions, and governmental systems. Reportedly, religion is lived and performed daily through rituals, routines, and habits. Positive thoughts, emotions, and actions that reflect God's goodness and mercy, result in forms of beneficent spirituality and religion. The opposite can be said of the warmongering Greco-Roman, who devised a system of worship to distract the masses from their true divine nature, by seeking a materialistic, Caucasian god for salvation.

Historically, Flavius Constantine, as well as other Greco-Romans have become the embodiment, and incarnation of the Caucasian god of salvation. To maintain their position of power and control, Constantine and the Presbyters, or council of Bishops would not divulge and convey confidential information that can be internalized and lived to yield mass spiritual and mental liberation. To maintain their elite, initiate status all others including laymen or taxpaying subjects and slaves must never experience aspects of spiritual liberation. For the uninitiated masses, paying taxes, tribute, and acquisition of material possessions cannot provide spiritual clarity or clairvoyant solutions to life's challenges. Experiences of clarity and clairvoyance require commitment and devotion to meditation, yoga, and Qi Gong to shift the flow of internal energies to yield healing, for example. Most of humankind requires mental, emotional, and physical healing. However, before this can occur, sincerity and personal forgiveness, as well as forgiveness of others are prerequisites.

In addition to Jacobovici's film documentary, Joseph Atwell commits to precise and thorough analysis of the origin of Christianity. In Atwell's documentary: "*History of Christianity - How Christianity was invented,*" the narrator says the following:

> . . . historians and scholars have shown that the Gospels were not the product of illiterate, Jewish fishermen, rather, they are a sophisticated literary work combining religious ideas of the day, with Roman political perspective and power. Joseph Atwell's research reveals that reading the works of Flavius Josephus concurrently with the New Testament shows that the events of Jesus' life were not historical, but rather, all of them are dependent on the events and military campaign of Titus Flavius. Jesus Christ was an allegory for the Roman Caesar, Titus: The Messiah of the Roman empire. The Roman son of a god that Christianity was established, or setup to worship.

Clear, decisive, and unbiased research attempts to show that the Caucasian god depicts Caesar, and Greco-Roman leadership syphoning energy and taxes from the masses to feed their ever-growing ego, and tremendous desire for worship. The origins of Christianity may be also found in the Ptolemaic mystery cult that venerated, or co-opted the Neter (god) Hapis, or Apis bull symbology of ancient Memphis, Egypt (Kemet). The Greco-Roman may have taken the bull symbology of Hapis, or Apis and transfigured it into the slaughter, and bloodletting of the sacrificial bull of Mithras and Mithraism.

Asiatic or Persian, and Greco-Roman Occupation of Ancient Egypt (Kemet): A Perversion of African Knowledge of Creation and Purpose

Hundreds of years prior to the Roman Caesars, Titus, and Flavius Constantine, approximately in 332 BCE, the Greeks or Ptolemy occupied Kemet, or ancient Egypt. Some might argue that the Persians assimilated into ancient Egyptian (Kemetic) culture forming an Egypto-Persian syncretism prior to the Greeks. This is true, but, whether Greco-Persian, or Greco-Egyptian, the Ptolemy did not practice positive spirituality through priestly kingship. Initially, Ptolemaic occupation was purely militaristic, and disinterested in a positive lifestyle that practices the intricacies of occult, spiritual ritual, initiation, and ceremony. Their primary concern was empirical, tangible reality and physical power to establish a fascist dynasty of military dominance. Secondly, to secure their place of relative empirical superiority, and spiritual worship or veneration as a god, Ptolemy I, or Soter (Savior) created a new syncretism depicting the ancient Neter, Ausar (Osiris), with Greek, Persian, and Caucasian aquiline features.

Symbolic of the Hapis or Apis personality cult of ancient Egypt (Kemet) is a bull and its horns representing virulence, and sexual prowess. Today, some traditional cultures use deer antler velvet or powder as a metabolic enhancer, or aphrodisiac. In many depictions, wedged between the bullhorns is a Sun disk, or Ra, symbolizing the lifeforce or holy spirit. Also, a correct understanding of creation reveals that approximately 13.9 billion-years-ago, God's consciousness and spirit emanated from an explosion to create all things in existence. While in trance or meditation, practitioners can envision or imagine the rays of the Sun (Ra), causing a sensation of peaceful and joyful delight or comfort, sustainable through all of life's endeavors. Practitioners manifest peace and sustained joy (happiness), as reflections of the holy spirit to allow God to enter and remain in their lives.

The shared imagery of a bull, such as Apis from Kemet also transitions into Mithraic symbolism. The bull, slaughtered in a bloodletting motif can represent the loss of innocent lives during Persian, and Greco-Roman occupation, akin to other military invasions. The Apis bull of Memphis and Kemet can represent virile African-spiritual practices, contrasted by the people who were sacrificially slaughtered, also symbolized through this bloodletting motif. In the antediluvian, prehistoric, or Ausarian paradigm humankind willfully chose to strive to achieve divinity, and to be one with God, The Creator of all things. Through occupation of Africa and cultural assimilation, Persians and Greco-Romans, or the Ptolemaic empire dismantled Ausarianism and restructured it into a materialist, shallow framework reflecting the worship of Caesar, governmental systems, and a Caucasian god with aquiline features.

In the ancient Egyptian (Kemetic) narrative Set cut his brother, Ausar's, body into 14 pieces, but this act of violence is not the central motif, unlike the bloodletting of the sacrificial bull in Mithraism, and the crucifixion of Christ. These images of bloodletting apparently reinforce and justify crimes against humanity, as a type of negative natural order and ritual: the warring, ritualistic slaughter of the spiritually evolved daughters and sons of God, as well as the uninitiated daughters and sons of men.

During occupation of ancient Kemet, approximately in 305 BCE, Ptolemy I, or Soter, formed a new socio-religious syncretism, the Serapis (Apis) Christos (Christ) cult. An etymological analysis of the title or term, Christ, reveals the following: The ancient Greek term for Christ is *khristos*. In Latin, however, *Christus* is the word for Christ. The ancient Hebrew translation of the terms (*khristos* and *Christus*) is *mashiah* or *Messiah*. The previously mentioned terminologies are noun forms of the verbal adjective for *khriein*, or *chrism* meaning to rub, or anoint. Most importantly, the Greco-Roman terms, *Christus*, and *khristos,* both refer to the anointing process, a form of blessing during religious ceremonies, where oil is rubbed into the skin. The Old English term *Hæland* or healer, and savior is the preferred description for Jesus, however.

Following the syncretic model, prior to Serapis Christos and Ptolemy I, or Soter, a Kemetic (ancient Egyptian) priestly cult, with membership living an esoteric, stoic life had to exist. Greek, Latin, and Hebrew descriptions of the title, Christ, are reminiscent of the ancient, priestly lifestyle of members of this Kemetic (ancient Egyptian) socio-religious tradition. In the Kemetic custom individuals induce states of deep meditative trance, while anointing themselves, and others with aromatic oils (*Christus)* to balance the life force, Ra, Qi body and spirit. Meditation, and rubbing anointing oils into Qi meridians, or energy channels releases blockages and stagnation, thus the life force can flow throughout the body to induce physical, mental, and emotional healing.

Additionally, healing provided a conduit for release from religiosity and propaganda that justified occupation by Persian, and Greco-Roman emperors, generals, and politicians, who enforced their will on others through forms of imperialistic-military strategy and invasion. To establish a hegemonic relationship, where subjects begin to accept that imperial elitists' domination is in natural and divine order, regional socio-religious narratives and literature must support godlike domineering personalities. To maintain order, and to lessen the possibility of mass uprisings, a Greco-Egyptian, and then a Greco-Roman syncretism emerged. Imperial fascist-world leaders were worshipped as spiritual figureheads with divine rights. False history and incorrect beliefs may explain the contemporary socio-religious narrative of the second coming of Christ, who died as a spiritual figurehead, but will return as a world leader to enforce God's will, by redeeming and saving the righteous. Again, this narrative is maintained to detain mass perpetual hope, to ensure that people will never empower themselves through spiritual science to positively impact, and economically boycott the empirical powerbase of global control.

Chapter Eight

Trance Induction to Supplicate the Spiritual Realm for Assistance

A realistic and honest approach to life events should conclude that meditative-trance practices, and forms of self-hypnosis are often inextricably linked to accomplishing real-world, mundane physical activities. Within the etymology of the word meditation is the prefix mid or middle: A state of awareness between being asleep and awake. In this meditative state, spirit, or energy is cultivated, strengthened, and harnessed to transition into willfully directed actions to accomplish real-time, and real-world objectives.

Reasoning similarly, ritual is habitual behavior, such as daydreams for some people. While in the meditative state of daydreams, there exists an analogous experience of the trance-state between sleep and wakefulness. Often during momentary daydreams, however, specific events or occurrences etched in the mind are subsequently re-enacted in real-time, and real-world situations. This is a shared experience for most people identified as spiritual, secular, atheistic, or religious.

Mental, spiritual, or psychic methods are also employed to transition desire (a strong yearning or want for something) into convictions, such as the relentless need to dominate and subjugate others through conquest and occupation. To subjugate others, during ceremony and ritual, Greco-Roman elites may have envisioned themselves as the victorious, warrior-god Mithras, often depicted as an initiate wearing a Phrygian cap. This ceremonial practice was possibly utilized to garner the psychic power embodied in the energies of Mithras, prior to embarking on the battlefield, as well as other real-world situations. Likewise, for the Mithraic elite, the outcome of mundane life events could have been influenced through visualizations, symbolism, and determined self-actualization.

While stilled or immobile, mantras, and hekau, as well as repetitive visualization of the same life event, enhances the imaginative faculty during meditation and prayer to invoke the powers of the spirit. Bodily vessels used to accomplish specific goals on this physical plane, become enthralled by this spiritual and psychic experience. Then power (emotion and energy) is harnessed to mobilize the physical vehicle into action to impact real-life events. Mithras is bold and active, rather than meek and mild: A soldier, not a shepherd. A warrior, who literally takes the bull, or Apis by the horns. He then slaughters the animal by stabbing it in the torso, spilling blood, which redesigns the universe in the image of a Greco-Roman god. Occasionally, in this bloodletting motif a dog symbolizing Sebek, Anubis, or Set consumes the blood of the Apis bull - the eternal peace and joy (happiness) of the Black African.

Before and during the Ptolemaic occupation of ancient Egypt (Kemet) and Africa, Persians and Greco-Romans studied, were initiated into, or commissioned priests and other spiritual scientists to do their bidding. A similar syncretism occurred to form the Mithras personality type, and most of the borrowed, ancient gods of the Roman Imperial Cult, who exhibit aspects of angelic energies that can be cultivated and invoked through prayer and meditation, to gain personal power to accomplish successes in life. Initiates familiarized themselves with the telltale characteristics of individual gods of the Roman pantheon, allowing for recognition of godlike personifications exhibited through certain people. As Christianity took root in Rome, presumably people who displayed particular qualities during their religious tenure, were also beatified at the time of death: exalted as saints, then called upon by parishioners to gain insight, when confronted with challenging situations. The contrast for the Abrahamic xenophobe and Christian apologist is that these saints of monotheistic Catholicism, also, truthfully serve a similar purpose as the gods of the polytheistic Roman pantheon, as well as the deities of Hinduism, Orisha of West African traditions, and the Neteru of Kemetic spirituality, to name a few.

Ausarianism, Mithraism, Catholicism, and Christianity

Compared to Mithraism, an elitists' cult comprising Roman generals, belief in Christianity has greater appeal; its message was one of relative acceptance and embrace of the common man. At her death, Constantine's mother was beatified to become Saint Helena: one of the first female iconic figures of

Christendom. Not beatified, however, were Christian Bishops, businessmen, merchants, and soldiers in Constantine's army, although he, himself, was not a convert. Constantine's organizational efforts to wield physical power by shaping a brand of emperor as both a Christian and fascist-world leader was such a success that approximately 65-years after the council of Nicaea, in 390 CE, Mithraism came under attack by the newly organized Christian church.

Another term for these Christians would be Roman mercenaries, who were essentially employed by, or carrying out the will of the emperor, and Bishops. Referring to them as Christians contradicts the passivistic, meek and mild comportment of Christ who would not motivate the mob to attack Mithraic enclaves. Fascist-world leadership figuratively, or symbolically representing positive-spiritual cultivation is also an oxymoron, since spiritual leadership implies a person, or people who emulate the image and likeness of God. By God's goodness, mercy, and grace: The Creator of all things is not a negative-fascist entity, emitting energies for the sole purpose of physical and mental control through conquest, murder, and chattel slavery. This is the work of humankind, who has the freedom to choose.

The organizational success of the Council of Nicaea rallied Roman Catholic or Christian mercenaries, conscripts, and citizens around a banner of deception, perpetrated by elites, who stem from the Ptolemaic tradition and empire. Deception, in that the Asiatic Hittites, Habiru, and then Greco-Romans from the Ptolemaic bloodline co-opted African-spiritual traditions, by transforming Ausar into Osiris. Ausar's (Kemetic and African) physical and spiritual attributes were altered to fit the Serapis Christos, and Christ Jesus personality type, with aquiline or Caucasian features. Preceding this, African people's life purpose, including common women and men, was achieving the highest level of consciousness through spiritual evolution, characteristic of others who had attained the title of Ausar.

In Rome, however, elites who garnered mass control and manipulation, may have felt that the noble rites of Mithras were too similar to forms of their contrived religious syncretism of Christian veneration. Modern historians remain challenged to find authentic, archeological evidence that verifies and corroborates the existence of this globally acclaimed historical figure, Christ Jesus, whose death 2,021 years ago ushered in the common era. Civilizations that predate Catholicism: Mesoamerican, African, Egyptian (Kemetic), Sumerian, Babylonian, and East Asian were meticulous record keepers, who provide primary-source evidence of historical figures and events.

It is unusual that authentic, primary-source evidence of an historical Jesus is lacking from the annals of current-Western societies that pride themselves on meticulous record keeping and celebration of Greco-Roman heritage. The rational for this lack of evidence is that the physical character, an historic Jesus did not impact the ancient Greco-Roman and Hebrew world. This lacking impact in the form of historic evidence brings into question the miraculous Biblical events of Jesus. Surly, if Biblical events are an accurate, literal documentation of New Testament occurrences, instead of compilations of revived embellishments, there would be much greater primary-source, archeological evidence.

Nonetheless, to destroy historical evidence that Catholics borrowed from other competing spiritual systems, Roman mercenaries or the Christian mob, systematically attacked and destroyed statues depicting the epic of Mithras, while defacing other iconography. Archaeological evidence from the last known Mithraic temple dates to approximately 408 CE. Mithraeums, or Roman temples venerating the Mithraic mysteries, were in most ancient European countries: Britain, Spain, Germany, and other regions of Europe and North Africa.

Compared to Mithraic teachings and philosophy, a contemporary-spiritual counter narrative is not one of taking control of life, but instead, parishioners have faith and believe that the soul will be saved through prayer, and a plea for redemption, irrespective of a positive or negative lifestyle. Within this labyrinth of deception, accountability, ownership, and power are wrested from the individual and placed in the hands of this Greco-Roman god. In this version of a spiritual relationship, shepherds are passive, but sheep are far more docile and incapable of critical thought and problem solving. Again, shepherds are gods, but sheep are docile animals, controlled and led by their simple, emotional nature.

Symbolically, humans must emulate the docile nature of sheep. Energies or emotions are cultivated to achieve docility, which brings about passive, or sheepish behaviors originating from the less evolved midbrain: the limbic or mammalian brain. This is the central processing unit for mammalian learning and emotional responses. When spontaneous responses to critical-life events are based on emotions, instead of slow, methodical-critical thinking, societies can be controlled.

In the modern era, official government narratives of life altering events, such as September 11, 2001, and other so-called terror attacks are broadcasted via corporate-controlled media outlets. Instead of citizens using critical thought and scientific inquiry to question government and corporate narratives, they react with an emotional, spontaneous response to support invading foreign territories to manipulate and control the natural resources of others. Reminiscent of the Roman Christian mob, but eventually prosecuted and convicted for numerous crimes against the state, certain sheepish and sycophantic Caucasian Americans sort the protection of White privilege, while attacking the nation's capital on January 6th, 2021.

Furthermore, elitist leadership functions to preserve its place of privilege by wielding subtle, psychic influence, empirical, physical, and spiritual power designed to maintain mass control, while continuing to monopolize and reap tremendous profit from exploiting global natural resources and tax paying citizens. Most nationalistic, government, corporate, religious, and media indoctrination functions to mislead, miseducate, and control through deception, so that elites can maintain their place of physical power and privilege.

Historically aligned to the acquisition of power and control, Constantine and the Presbyters borrowed from the qualities and attributes of preexisting gods. They, according to Ms. French who mentions critical information from the "Historia Ecclesiastica", narrowed the names of their new gods from fifty-three to five. Of the five gods being debated, this literature focuses on three: Mithras, Krishna, and Heru

(African) or Horus (Greco-Roman). As a reminder, recall the historical backdrop of personality, or energy veneration of the Indo-Iranian, or Persian god Mitra, stemming from at least 1,500 BCE. Later Mitra became Mithras, and its energies and archetypal personality were invoked throughout Rome, and Roman held territories. Remaining to be discussed, however, are two gods: Krishna, and Heru or Horus. Emphasis is on these three: Mithras, Krishna, and Heru or Horus, whose transformative energies were manipulated to shape the only begotten son, or a literal, Caucasian god known as the spiritual, Jesus Christ of organized Catholicism.

Krishna, Conventional Science, and God's Consciousness

The name or title Christ sounds very similar to Krishna, who is seemingly one of the gods debated at the Council of Nicaea. Krishna is a historical person or figure who preceded Christ by at least 3,000 years. Krishna appeared on Earth 5,000 years ago, in India. For one hundred and twenty-five years, he led an exemplary life as he communed with humankind. He is described as the godhead, or supreme personality, who simultaneously expresses six different attributes: *Wealth, power, fame, beauty, wisdom, and renunciation*. It is *renunciation* that places Krishna as a spiritual figurehead or godhead. The five other attributes: *Wealth, power, fame, beauty, and wisdom* can be assessed within a worldly context, and may describe elitist leadership.

The positive-spiritual attributes of *wealth, power, fame, beauty, and wisdom* are expressed only through *renunciation* of egotistical, sensual, and selfish desires. Although possibly lacking in material possessions, spiritual *wealth, power, and wisdom* result in experiences of eternal peace and joy (happiness). Power does not discriminate. Spiritual power can be either positive or negative, depending on the individual, or group mindset and dynamic, resolved to bring into fruition a specific intent, expectation, or event. Expressions of positive-spiritual power are connected to God, and bring no harm to individuals, the environment or nature. In the contemporary era, however, negativity is pervasively expressed in the form of greed and selfishness. If left unchecked, negative impulsivity eventually causes harm to the individual, as well as nature, and the entire Homo sapien sapien species.

Living truth exemplifies meaningful positive behavior: God's purpose for creating the universe is so It can enter, grow, and share life experiences through Its creations. As such, humankind can be further empowered by prioritizing life's purpose, which should be to reflect God's goodness, mercy, and love. Through spiritual practices that integrate love, or the ability to share without expecting anything in return, divine or higher states of consciousness are also experienced. Emulating the elitist's model established by most global leadership results in a human, who is extremely lacking in love and positive spirituality, however. To control mass populations and the species at large, negative world leadership and elitists also use class and race warfare, along with other divide and conquer strategies. These previous descriptions of human negative emotionalism are in complete opposition to Krishna's positive spiritual agenda.

To further understand this positive, spiritual awareness or consciousness stemming from God and the creation of the universe, a biological example is most appropriate. Western biological, and empirical science says that *the whole is greater than the sum of its parts.* Meaning, for example, that individual cell parts, or organelles, can be studied in isolation to gain greater understanding of their function in relationship to the entire cell. Organelles, such as mitochondria, are sites of energy production or cellular respiration. DNA resides in the nucleus, which is an organelle that directs all cell activities, specifically protein production and cell division. In the previous examples: *the sum of the parts* can be all organelles working together for the wellbeing of the entire cell, which is *the whole.*

A simplistic and inadequate attempt to explain the greatness, or elusive nature of *the sum of the parts,* seems to suggest that as cell organelles communicate with each other, an intelligent, synergistic relationship develops, culminating in proper cell function. It is the elusive, or hidden nature of this intelligence that makes it great. In simple terms, Western science does not truly know how cell organelles function. Neither does it know the origin of this intelligence, or its synergistic effects. What Western science does is develop models, or schema, to explain the steps, or striations of specific processes. This explains the meaning of the phrase: *The whole is greater than the sum of its parts.* The processes executed by the *sum of the parts*, or organelles, are rather elusive, and cannot be fully explained by Western science.

This phrase: *The whole is greater than the sum of its parts* is their best attempt to explain God's consciousness that disseminates from the creation of the universe 13.9 billion-years-ago. Western empirical scientists imply that this elusive, synergistic intelligence exists, but are unwilling to implore their spirit to navigate the hidden recesses of this consciousness, dwelling within, and directing *the sum of the parts,* resulting in proper functioning of the *whole.* This same intelligence directs all universal phenomena, such as covalent and ionic-electron bonding to create physical matter.

Unless consciousness – awareness of the proper functioning of all things in the universe that stems from God – is considered, this theoretical framework through which organelles communicate to maintain homeostasis, and health or balance within a cell, is not precisely articulated. Without acknowledging consciousness, the following questions remain unanswered: How does the cell know the proper time to divide or reproduce? How did they develop a mechanism for cell division through mitosis and meiosis? How did the universal DNA sequence of adenine binding to thymine (A-T), and cytosine binding to guanine (C-G) evolve? How do single-celled organisms, such as protists, know to search their environment for food? How do photosynthetic cells know to make their own food? With these questions, and the study and practice of consciousness elevation comes an understanding that *the whole is no greater than the sum of its parts,* and vise-versa, since there is an omnipresent intelligence, which is the unifier, maintaining divine order.

A more eclectic approach combines conventional science with spiritual traditions to assert that in the beginning, 13.9 billion-years-ago, there was a singularity (all of one thing), or void that became conscious or self-aware. In other words, as The Creator Being became conscious of Its own consciousness: It knew that it existed. Being a singularity of pure consciousness: nothing else existed. Therefore, The Creator

Being was alone. At that moment, It willed to have experiences through other things, so it condensed, then exploded, causing Its conscious awareness and spirit (energy) to differentiate, forming all things in existence. From that initial explosion, energy travels in spirals to collide and form physical matter. God differentiates into energy and matter so that It can have experiences through Its creations. This phenomenon occurs so that God will no longer be alone (a singularity, or all of one thing). Emanating from that explosion is an expanding universe stabilized by God's consciousness, which is the proper order guiding all things in creation.

Consciousness is the adhesive, or order that binds, and unites all things. It is the organizational structure that maintains a functional universe. Ancient-spiritual science commands a more comprehensive understanding of consciousness, and the superior lifeform from which it originates. Evidence of a more advanced and holistic science takes the form of ancient people being able to produce global-megalithic temples and pyramids, which perpetually harmonize Earth's cosmic energies, even in these moments of chaos and uncertainty. Modern science cannot explain the construction of these pyramids and temples, neither can it replicate these megalithic accomplishments.

To the contrary, labeling spiritual science, or the study of different forms of flowing energies throughout the universe and biological organisms as Vodun, Voodoo, and superstition steers mass populations away from the liberating, power rendering and transformative experiences of this metaphysical discipline. On the surface, because conventional science seeks to appear atheistic and rational, unlike the irrational Roman Catholic church that dominated during the European dark ages,

Western academia does not integrate spiritual disciplines for enhanced experiences of the awesome attributes of God's consciousness. Instead, conventional science simply proclaims that life is not fully understood, and *the whole is greater than the sum of its parts.*

As alluded to previously, if most people were circumspect of religious dogma, while studying the life of Christ, including his lessons and sermons, they may conclude that he is a spiritual archetype, not led or consumed by emotions. A quality of Christ making him a savior god is an introspective life that can be emulated to set the captives free from negative-emotional suffering. Undeniably, Christ spent extensive hours and days in meditation. He spent at least forty days meditating in the wilderness: engaging breathing techniques to remain fixed on enhanced mental images, and symbols during altered states of elevated consciousness to initiate change. One purpose of this process is nourishing the spirit with mental images, symbols, and hekau (words of power), while envisioning appropriate, positive responses to life challenges. This is a protracted, ongoing process where daily meditations, and other practices are integral in realizing that life experiences are spiritual, teachable moments that have the potential to free the soul from negative-emotional suffering.

Chapter Nine

Maya: In Opposition to Nurturing and Cherishing Eternal Peace and Joy

The terms Krishna consciousness, and even Christ consciousness are specific phrases for the more general concept of God's consciousness. For simplicity's sake, Krishna consciousness is God's consciousness, or the inherent ability to understand, realize, and live the purpose of creation. The intent of creation is for humankind to reflect and emulate God's image and likeness through Its goodness, mercy, and love. The subtleties here are that specific qualities and experiences of Amen (eternal peace), Nebertcher (Lord of All), and God (The Supreme Being) are hidden and imperceptible to most, except an initiated few. Most people have not matured enough to utilize the correct prescriptive lens to know that God is visible in all things, since all things were created by It. This is what it means to be a creationist, as well as having a holistic view and understanding of creation, itself. For male patriarchies and Abrahamic traditions that celebrate segregative-analytical thinking, along with war, and socio-religious, political, and economic domination for mass control, it is challenging to know and experience God's existence in all things.

Socio-religious indoctrination, and global miseducation have the debilitating effect of deterring people from cultivating a spiritual relationship with God, through higher levels of consciousness, and psychic experiences. To control Africa's abundance of natural resources, and to manipulate the spiritual power of its indigenous people, this region has been targeted for colonialization and exploitation. Abrahamic, socio-religious indoctrination, which in many cases was forced on African people, is also a historic hegemonic tool to support, justify, and celebrate colonial despotic behavior. Implicit to the contemporary narrative of history is that the colonizers are a civilizing force, bringing culture and humanity to a devil-worshiping, barbaric, and savage race of Africans. Even today, the European nation of France, and others continue to control the financial institutions and policy of former African colonies. France collects taxes and colonial reparations, thereby depriving specific African nations from funding and controlling their own national destiny, through infrastructure development and socio-economic progress.

For Africans on the continent, and those of the diaspora, the path or portal to experience liberation, and higher levels of awareness is through celebration, and practice of certain ritual traditions frowned upon by Abrahamic socio-religious dogma. Ignorant colonial bystanders observing these ancient customs are unaware and oblivious to forms of ancestral, holistic, divination rituals. Bystanders in observance of Black

African, traditional-ritualistic practices and ceremony are often oblivious of the impactful, life altering effect of specific celebrations that knit together entire communities through trance induction, ancestral spirit possession, dance, drumming, love, and the sharing of food.

Outside of insolated indigenous communities, mass populations are kept under control through fear and ignorance perpetuated by government institutions, as well as corporate influences and organized religious indoctrination. So that people continue to follow those with an opulent and self-centered lifestyle, control through fear and ignorance are rationalized by Maya, or the illusion of happiness from material possessions and excess. The unspoken truth is that control through fear, also, results in inhibition of experiences of mental and spiritual liberation to access the imperceptible nature of oneness with God.

An experience of Hinduism's Maya, as possibly understood and taught by Lord Krishna, can be the illusion that happiness is primarily influenced by external factors, such as material possessions and relationships with others. Peace (Amen) and eternal happiness are internally nourished by an elusive relationship with an indwelling God. The atheist might agree with the previous statement. However, instead of mentioning an indwelling God, atheistic descriptions might speak of relationships with an internal, peaceful consciousness that came into existence 13.9 billion-years-ago. Nonetheless, Maya or the illusion of happiness from the accumulation of material possessions is the elitists' method of control, since they manipulate the printing and distribution of fiat currency. Through the illusion of happiness by corporate-controlled media, people are highly motivated to follow elites, who accumulate excessive amounts of fiat currency. This illusionary lifestyle of excessive materialism results in both groups: elites and mass populations experiencing a severe lack of internal peace and eternal joy (happiness).

In the modern era, most media, especially commercials with the intended purpose of promoting mindless consumerism, portrays members of upper and middle-income societies as having material, physical, and tangible wealth. Characters live in stable suburban or urban communities. They own modern cars parked in front of homes that appear relatively well kept. Alternatively, they might live in a decorative apartment with modern amenities.

In other forms of programming, even if portrayed as experiencing periods of mild emotional distress, characters always recover from these challenges. Mainstream media promotes the following subtle, subliminal, or hidden messages: Tax-paying upper and middle-income earners can overcome distress and acquire happiness due to education and income levels, intellectual prowess, socio-economic status, or a network of family, friends, and acquaintances. In general, these upstanding-tax-paying citizens seem to be experiencing a sort of bliss, without any apparent affinity to spiritual insight.

In other words, higher levels of education, intellect, and material wealth stand in place of authentic spiritual practices, which can make life more holistic and endearing. Authentic, in that prerequisites for spiritual life are positive, loving thoughts and action, coupled with a willingness to share verifiable, truthful information, and material possessions. This exemplifies selflessness, since it is sharing regardless of religious persuasion, social class, or race (phenotypic characteristics).

On the other hand, selfishness is so pervasively promoted in modern-mainstream society that often media characters are self-centered, but never portrayed as unbalanced and experiencing excessive emotional stress, or overwhelming distress. They remain blissful due to the comforts of material possessions. They do not worry and are not concerned with bills, unruly children, drug and alcohol addiction, or COVID-19, which are realities for global populations, irrespective of Maya.

Mainstream media also programs into human-mass consciousness experiences of Maya that promote the misconception that the accumulation of material wealth brings power and happiness through liberty to do whatever is physically desired. For those who lack emotional control and discipline, Maya, along with media and government programming can result in a spiritual void, lacking in eternal peace and joy. This void or emptiness cannot be satisfied through negative-emotional behavior, or alcohol, and addictive substance abuse. However, those with material wealth, often, must still conform to secular laws. Money and material possessions are not essential ingredients to make fine, upright, and moral citizens. Whether by noble birth, race (White privilege), or diligent work and effort, many wealthy people may be morally bankrupt, although they control most of Earth's resources. Moral bankruptcy and deficiency are evident in their lack of love, compassion for others, and spiritual practices deeply rooted in the psyche of indigenous people.

Another major form of Maya is the concept of race. As mentioned, and possibly taught in the law curriculum of Critical Race Theory (CRT), genotypically, or on the molecular level of genes, race does not exist. There are genes that code for specific physical characteristics, or a phenotype. On this planet, all known biological organisms possess genes that code for phenotypic traits. Evidence of gene coding is universal for all life on the planet, not just for Homo sapien sapiens. Glucose regulatory genes are shared among different organisms as disparate as plants and humans, for example.

In both scholarly disciplines: biology, and CRT that studies biased laws and court decisions against marginalized Black people, race does not exist. However, the mental and emotional trauma of systemic racism are realized, due to individuals in position of physical power, who enforce prejudicial policies and decisions from within institutions in favor of White supremacy and privilege. Using contemporary terminology to describe wild and domesticated animals, no other organisms are relegated to specific racial groups. There is no race of elephants, sheep, cows, or giraffes, for example. Race is a socio-economic construct that was designed by elites to divide, conquer, and control mass populations, who disregard experiences of shared exploitation as with the middleclass tax burden.

Based on phenotypic characteristics, people are made to identify with one group over another. Politicians, government officials, or negative-spiritual leadership often have a tremendous influence on people, specifically soldiers to commandeer resources from other vulnerable groups. Race is also an ideological entity constructed for socio-economic manipulation and competition. The concept of race was developed so that groups with specific phenotypic characteristics, such as aquiline features, are always ahead in this competition. These groups often lack positive-spiritual practices, but they have the strongest desire for acquiring material possessions. They are also willing to decimate nature for profit and material gain, while causing the physical, and psycho-spiritual enslavement of others through low-level transubstantiation rituals, and media propaganda that helps to induce fear and mass hysteria.

Again, the Hindu understanding of Maya can be forms of delusion or illusion that are predominantly derived from stimulating the five senses, which forms a denser, more physical or tangible, empirical reality. These stimuli are easily manipulated by elitists, who control the media and distribution of fiat currency. In contrast to Maya, and perversions of reality, empirical science using *The Double-slit Experiment* has shown that expectation, awareness, or consciousness have an underlying effect on the flow of energy particles, causing them to behave more like physical matter. In other words, as evident through their megalithic accomplishments and metaphysical practices, prehistoric and antediluvian societies knew that on the subatomic level of particles, consciousness can influence energy flow to have it behave and function as precursors to physical matter.

An assessment of quantum physics and *The Double-slit Experiment* begs the questions: Do all things, animate and inanimate, have a consciousness of their own? On the subatomic level, is consciousness, also, a particle that can interact with energy flow to influence the formation of physical matter? Is it that the observer's consciousness interacts with that of energy flow to influence and shape its behavior to form physical matter? Is the function of energy flow, itself, to allow for the influence of consciousness to shape, and direct the creation of physical matter, and other occurrences? The previous questions and possibilities seem to define creation, given that The Supreme Being differentiates into all things, by subdividing Its spirit (energy) and conscious awareness (self).

Initiates into intuitive, metaphysical science may be unaware of empirical evidence from *The Double-Slit Experiment* but they still often choose to function within an accessible, but refined and ethereal version of reality to gain greater access to divine, ancestral insight, during communication rituals. During trance induction for ancestral communication and healing, consciousness affects the spirit to generate physiological benefits. In the contemporary era, through ritual and mediumistic trance, positive ancestral energies can also be cultivated to support the realization that God's consciousness and divinity dwells in all things, including humankind. Mediumistic trance experiences can assist with acknowledging ancient, and contemporary African accomplishments, making the initiate proud of ancestral relationships that transcend time and space. Further, related research into the *Double-Slit Experiment,* or the measurement mistake of quantum physics, has shown that meditators or people who induce a state of trance, have a greater impact on energy flow to manifest changes in physical reality.

Accessing Knowledge and Information Stored in DNA to Restore Ancient, Spiritual Magnificence

Unlike ancestral-communication rituals where participants attempt to gain answers and clarity to specific life challenges, modern archeology tends to choose to promote Maya by not acknowledging specific pieces of evidence from ancient civilizations. Certain religious belief systems also promote Maya through repetitive false narratives that are deficient in archeological fact. However, renowned British author and presenter, Graham Hancock, repudiates conventional archeology by discussing evidence from sunken cities off the coast of India, which substantiates the existence of Lord Krishna. One particular ancient city is deluged in the Gulf of Khambhat, where powerful crosscurrents make it nearly impossible to dive 170-feet to the bottom. At this site, human artifacts have been recovered, such as wood and pottery shards that date to approximately 32,000 years ago. This evidence directly contradicts mainstream archeology, which says that no cities existed at that time. Michael Cremo, author of "*Forbidden Archeology*" mentions that oceanographers conclude that the Gulf of Khambhat formed approximately 9,000 years ago, due to sea-level rise. This suggests that this city existed above sea-level for at least 23,000 years.

Similar to physical evidence proving that antediluvian cities are submerged underwater, ancestral knowledge that is encoded in DNA can also be retrieved. A basic scientific observation is relevant and shows that memories, and other implicit characteristics from ancestry are stored in inherited, genetic material, such as DNA and genes. When the eggs of specific species of nest-building birds are removed from nature, then hatched and raised in captivity, adult birds are still able to build similar, if not the same intricate nests, as their fore parents. Since these birds were not taught the skills of nest building by their predecessors, how was this information passed on as a functional part of their reproductive cycle? As evident in the bird's nest-building ability, memories and constructive, functional information, as well as knowledge are stored in DNA and genes from hundreds and thousands of years in the past. The semiconservative model of DNA replication during meiotic and mitotic cell division ensures that all, if not most lifeforms contain ancestral genetic information and genes.

To affect beneficial, positive change, knowledge can be retrieved or unlocked from within genetic information. During ritual, deep-meditative trance induction can activate ancestral DNA, and spiritual energies can be bestowed on initiates who, then, verbalize and share ancient information. These messages, and memories from ritual experiences can be retrieved outside of the event, in real-time, real-world situations to benefit initiates, and the larger society. In simple terms, when ancestral information is shared with communities, it is, now, the audience's responsibility to transition, implement, and live the message in real-world situations, outside of the ritual event. Similarly for humankind, information and knowledge to recreate great-ancestral civilizations and positive-spiritual culture are also stored within DNA.

Spiritual Traditions in Common Among Eastern, African, and Western Societies

Two-hundred miles northwest of the Gulf of Khambhat is the modern city of Dwarka. Archeologists, excavating modern Dwarka found signs of a settlement that was once inundated by the sea. While searching for more clues in only 70-feet of water off the coast of the existing city of Dwarka, divers uncovered a sandstone wall, cobblestone streets, and evidence of a prosperous seaport. Scholars declared these to be the remains of the ancient and legendary city of Dwarka. Ancient Hindu texts claim that this underwater, ancient city was the dwelling place of renowned Lord Krishna, a god held in high esteem throughout many Hindu traditions.

Not to be dismissed is archeological evidence, and the work of scholars that support the existence of the Hindu god Krishna. Due to religious dogma, and misinformation or incorrect belief that is not substantiated by scientific evidence, many groups discredit and exclude these findings from the narrative of human history.

Another peculiarity contrasting modern belief and ancient knowledge systems is the ancients' understanding that all of humankind has the potential to become true daughters and sons of God by adopting and cultivating a lifestyle that reflects God's spirit and consciousness, as well as Its image and likeness. In other words, God's goodness and mercy emanate and radiates from the lives of devotees and initiates, serving as Avatars and a conduit between the Neteru, ancients, deities, ancestors, spirits, or saints. The ancient and original purpose of humankind is to be initiated into specific knowledge systems to assist with fulfilling a lifestyle that practices celebration of ritualized meditation, yoga, Qi Gong, prayer, and hekau to reach higher states of consciousness, both individually and as a community.

The ancient, spiritually evolved daughters and sons of God used instruments and artifacts to assist with achieving and sustaining Godlike divinity, as they constructed magnificent temples to commune with God and the Neteru (Kemetic sacred personifications on the *Tree of Life*). All modern humans possess the same omnipresent, omnipotent, and omniscient qualities of God, but not in the same quantity, as discussed by the honorable Ra Un Nefer Amen, in the "*Metu Neter Vol I*". The Bible's New Testament says that Christ Jesus, or the only begotten son of God, was crucified, died, and ascended into the realm of the Father. In part, this describes Jesus' bodily resurrection. According to Christian tradition, the only begotten son of God, physically resides in heaven, where he is seated at the right hand of the Father. Deeply conflicted is the Western literal interpretation of spiritual, metaphysical science, which celebrates a physical being, once walking the face of Earth. The convoluted idea is that Jesus, with a body of flesh and blood, now resides in the recesses of heaven, in outer space, or on other worlds, without the use of life-support.

The metaphysical, and spiritual component of the Jesus narrative says that: Christ's holy spirit, or the comforter, is still accessible here on Earth to facilitate benevolent communication and continued salvation of humankind. Seemingly, interactions with the comforter, or holy spirit should enable Homo sapien sapiens, who may be spiritually evolved daughters and sons of God, to do even greater works than Christ Jesus, himself. These questions remain: If the comforter or Christ's holy spirit is accessible to all of humankind for transition from lower to higher levels of consciousness, why does Jesus need to return, as with the second coming? Are the methodologies and talent needed to engage the holy spirit being cultivated and shared with humankind, which will allow for greater works than Jesus? Is specific religious dogma and ignorance also inhibiting the species from fully embracing the holy spirit?

Viewing this resurrection narrative through a less xenophobic, but more inclusive and holistic lens, in the contemporary era, high-level initiates of the Nyingma, Buddhist sect also achieve ascension, or types of resurrection, at the time of death to form what is called the rainbow body. Buddha is also a title, and there are many ancient depictions and statues of people with the African phenotype, who have transcended to this higher level of conscious reality. Evolution in conventional academia describes the limited anatomical and physiological changes or advancement of Homo sapien sapien characteristics over the past 250,000 years, except for the sophisticated differences in the brain's prefrontal cortex. For some people, however, there is still consciousness elevation and spiritual evolution, quite possibly through Nyingma, rainbow body formation, and other esoteric practices and traditions. The point of contention is accessibility for common women and men, who can be spiritually evolving daughters and sons of God. For laypeople, or common women and men, ascension may have a more practical meaning, such as living life to its fullest, at this present moment. In simple terms, be mindful and ever-present during work, school, and when performing other mundane activities.

However, the African Abrahamic has been colonized through fear, and is programmed to receive suggestions to embrace socio-religious and political indoctrination, which can inhibit and suppress mental and spiritual liberation. Instead, negate these suggestions, whenever possible, by turning an inward, meditative eye, while becoming inspired through the breath to include esoteric practices into daily living. This does not result in demonic possession, but leads to a more holistic, balanced, and harmonious perspective of life.

A reality of this physical plane of existence is the need to earn a living, which tends to redirect energy resources, and deplete reserves that can be used for specific esoteric practices, such as Qi Gong, yoga, and ritualized meditation. Working for a living also results in less leisure to pursue esoteric practices, which are fulfilled by members of the Nyingma, Buddhist sect. For the African, and other practitioners, a balanced life that integrates ritualized meditation also elevates consciousness, thereby bringing the daughters and sons of God closer to realizing ascension in this lifetime. However, some xenophobic and misinformed followers of Christ would refer to Buddhists' rainbow body formation as evil, and the work of the devil, despite the zealous dialogue and celebration of afterlife ascension in Christian traditions.

Chapter Ten

Systemic Programming to Indoctrinate Negativity, While Inhibiting Connections to Spiritual Reality and Truth

Comparing certain Eastern and African socio-religious traditions and practices to achieve mental and spiritual liberation, there has been historic deception by dynastic generals, politicians, and emperors of the Greco-Roman military empire. Mass populations are being continually misguided through deception, distraction, and misdirection, so that clarity is not reached to realize that elites are entrenched in the business of self-service and self-dealing to secure positions of power and control. Examples of this are Flavius Constantine and the Council of Nicaea forcibly misleading humankind to adopt Christianity, while affirming themselves as incarnates of the only, true, son of God. The Council of Nicaea seemingly was a socio-religious, or ecumenical convention, which also had ties to patriarchal inheritance through Greco-Roman war and conquest. Patriarchal inheritance in the sense that throughout history, religion, politics, and violence have intermarried via pillaged war treasures bestowed and passed on within the bloodline of Emperors, Bishops, and other socio-political leadership. This patriarchal tradition of war also supports socialized gender discrimination, given that women often did not dispense, but were the victims of rape, slaughter, and carnage.

An extension of this historic state of war and conquest moves into the contemporary era, where soldiers, mostly men, earn the right to be militaristic priests, and Christ incarnate, transubstantiating the holy eucharist from bread into flesh, and wine into blood. These rituals may have the real purpose of rationalizing acceptance and tolerance of imperial leadership, by celebrating symbolic cannibalism, as well as war and sacrificial genocide. Partake in this holy sacrament.

The legacy of Greco-Roman patriarchy, and imperial violence transitions to contemporary societies in the form of neo-colonialism and imperialism, which programs the mind and spirit to accept that there is only one, true, son of God, incarnated in the embodiment of fascist-world leadership. This militaristic personality describes the Messiah for Hebrews. Oddly enough, this warring, socio-religious leader also embodies the second coming of the Messiah for Christians. Shift, and move past the idea of the second coming of the Messiah to transform into the divine realization of self: The third coming of spiritually evolving daughters and sons of God in this present moment, and right now. There is no longer a need to fear Roman crucifixion, or neo-colonial persecution. Once fear is released, the entire Homo sapien sapien species will come to realize its divine oneness with God, and all members will embrace their designation as daughters and sons.

Neo-colonial, hegemonic relationships are not based on mutual respect. Instead, imperialistic leadership tends to cultivate fear-based relationships, so that they can continue to dominate their subjects and collect taxes. Internalization of a conceptualized Caucasian god, as savior, explains the African and diasporic need for acceptance by former European, colonial masters. In situations such as these, realization and achievement of godhood and divinity, in this lifetime, are very foreign and alien to ordinary people, or common women and men, who still envision their god as colonial masters. For colonized people, it is challenging to blend the physical reality of bondage with spiritual experiences of liberation, since historically, Africans have been on the receiving end of chattel-slave persecution, as well as Jim Crow laws and segregation. Inherently, African people know and experience intolerance or nonacceptance from former colonial masters, who are also the symbolic or figurative embodiment of their Caucasian and Arab saviors. If Africans are not tolerated by Caucasians, then, how can they be accepted by Jesus to live eternally with him?

Likewise, Africans generally venerate and wait for the return of the same god as White supremacists, Ku Klux Klan members, and White Evangelicals, who demonize and inflict genocide on pigmented people. This elitist premise and belief in the only begotten son of God, limits, and confines human relationships with The Creator to only a select few intermediaries, or intercessors. Deliberate deception and confusion as to what constitutes empirical, fascist-world leadership, as opposed to a paradigm of positive-spiritual guidance and acceptance, makes the possibility of realizing and achieving divinity more elusive, and fleeting for the uninitiated masses.

The intended goal of this literature is to further an understanding that for elites to maintain mass control, governmental, religious, financial, and educational systems have been deployed to restrict consciousness and awareness to physical levels of reality. This also limits the human ability to be godlike by piercing through, and rupturing the veil of empirical illusion, and deception to reveal higher forms of spiritual existence. Elitist-world leadership has masterminded systems and institutions, where they are worshipped as gods, who heavily manipulate and control their subjects, tax-paying citizens, or psychic, mental slaves being held captive by fear of eternal damnation, and terror attack.

To gain a deeper understanding of religious deception, which promotes the falsity that those of Greco-Roman and Caucasian ancestry are most spiritually evolved, chronological ties have been drawn connecting the syncretism of Roman Catholicism and Christianity, with that of Mithraism, and the Hindu god, Krishna. As mentioned previously, the strategically placed Magi-like statues, wearing the Phrygian cap on the Arch of Constantine, alludes to, and symbolizes virtuous, spiritual initiation as it may exist within all, if not most systems and practices intended to elevate consciousness. To clarify, the purpose of consciousness elevation is to bring about selfless actions that benefit others, and has an impactful, positive influence on communities, societies, and the world at large.

Cognitive Dissonance and Maya

Art and media have been used to manipulate and influence human mass consciousness, and energies – the ability to do work – to bring about a specific, desired event, or type of future, where global elites continue to physically dominate. In most instances, consciousness is molded and shaped to produce populations of psychic or mental slaves, who cling to deceptive, official narratives broadcasted through mass media. This methodology of deception is known as hiding in plain sight. Here is a type of cognitive dissonance. Although provided with concrete, scientific evidence that contradicts the official narrative, corporate-controlled media uses subtle, or subliminal forces to program and manipulate mass consciousness through the illusion of happiness from acquiring material possessions. Based on public information, there is no current technology that can cause combustible jet fuel to melt steel, or dustify (turn to dust) both steel and concrete, causing the twin towers to fall. Similarly, it was impossible for the bullet that struck Senator John Connelly to zigzag in midair. However, mass populations are programmed to follow disingenuous elites, who control war technology to commit genocide. They also control technology to destroy nature, while misappropriating Earth's resources to produce wealth for themselves, and a minuscule redistribution of capital to others.

In many instances, Maya gratifies rationalization of an inability to change and correct inappropriately programmed behavior. This, in turn, bolsters cognitive dissonance, regardless of primary-source evidence and fact. For example, art and symbolism on the Arch of Constantine celebrate

Roman-pagan history and religion, but this is severely contrasted with the 1520 CE religious narrative of Pope Julius II, who commissioned artist Raphael to paint Vatican walls, which tells of triumphant-Christian, or non-pagan victories at the Milvian Bridge. By 1520 CE, a fascist means of control was established by a hegemonic Roman Catholic church, which works closely with government to control the means to misappropriate and redistribute vast amounts of stolen physical wealth. One of the founding fathers of this hegemonic system of fascist control is Emperor, Flavius Constantine.

Throughout his life, or on his deathbed, there is no definitive evidence of Emperor Constantine converting to Christianity. Cognitive dissonance results from a manipulative propaganda machine of contemporary mass media, which promotes illusion, enchantment, and Maya to produce mental captives, or global populations who are distracted from positive, productive change, which includes spiritual liberation, evolution, and growth. Furthermore, can it be said that the historical backdrop of evidence affirms Roman Catholicism and Christianity as forms of syncretism derived from pagan traditions?

In the case of the Arch of Constantine, the symbolic, but real message through art may be to inform devotees and practitioners of occult science that spiritual liberation can be achieved through states of higher consciousness to fulfill life's intended purpose. In the affirmative, this is a lifestyle of divinity that reflects God's image and likeness, as well as Its mercy and love. Occult science also allows practitioners to rupture the veil of empirical deception, perpetrated by ruling elites.

Again, a conventional, scientific analogy can assist in explaining occult science. The compound-light microscope has as many as three-ocular lenses, with different magnifications, that allow users to peer into the world of microbes. A microscope is an empirical tool that amplifies the sense of sight. At least in the areas of microbiology and oncology, for example, this specific tool allows technicians to see more clearly. Provided with evidence, or facts, it is challenging to mislead or misdirect skilled technicians. The same is true of spiritual occultists. Through a specific lifestyle of meditation techniques: rhythmic lower-abdominal breathing, mantras, prayer, hekau, and Qi Gong, practitioners experience divinity and higher states of awareness, which are their forms of positive, life-affirming evidence. These rituals may result in experiencing God's eternal peace and joy (happiness) that cannot be corrupted by the promise of material wealth and sensual excess.

Metaphysical and Spiritual Experiences: Pushing the Margins of Conventional Science for Explanations of Destiny

For the uninitiated masses, who are offered forms of literal interpretations of religious doctrine, so that they remain psychic or mental slaves dependent on government, corporations, and other geopolitical institutions to redistribute physical wealth, it is important to understand that liberating, spiritual power does not discriminate. Do the esoteric work, which summons spiritual power. Institutionalized government and religious programming results in most of humankind being unaware, or unwilling to admit to their deep-seated desire for psychic abilities, or clairvoyance through occult experiences and knowledge acquisition. Assimilation into materialistic societies that overemphasize perceptions of reality through the lens of empirical stimulation, deadens desires to comprehend the supernatural. Employing measures to obtain clarity into the occult is not considered acceptable and normal, compared to so-called rational, conventional education and intellectual prowess.

The study of physics with its mathematical equations, proofs, and technological application is more readily accepted in conventional academia and mainstream societies. However, metaphysics with its biological, and spiritual-energy-based rituals and practices should not be shunned or dismissed. Both sciences: physics, and metaphysics are attempts to understand the origin of the universe and purpose of creation. Practitioners of ancient metaphysical science have a distinct advantage, however. They turn an inward eye to shatter the veil of empirical deception, while cultivating eternal peace and joy to cope with life's most pressing challenges.

Most of humankind has a desire for definitive and clear answers to life's most urgent challenges. The same is true for the occult, metaphysical practitioners who have experiences of clairvoyance. This may take the form of enabling their entire being to sense peace and clarity that originates from the inception of the universe, which offers insight into definitive solutions to contemporary challenges. In contrast, self-centered, myopic, and selfish experimentation into occult science and rituals can result in material gain for other practitioners. In this instance, the rule of karma, and the law of cycles apply. Egotistical, self-centered application of physics, and metaphysical science can result in very destructive consequences. Examples of this can be genocidal chattel slavery, civil wars, and world wars that use weapons of mass destruction to decimate the species, planet, and nature.

For the initiated few, the critical incentive for accomplishing spiritual work is to gain insight into destiny or God's purpose for creation. Meditation, in addition to divination using oracles, such as the I Ching, Ifa, and Metu Neter can support and affirm intuitive insight into destiny to reveal God's tailored plan for individuals. Oracle consultations become more effective when linked to meditation to hear from the conscience, or the indwelling voice of God. Humility, and willingness to change behavior, by submitting or adhering to spiritual laws that require peace and oneness with God, along with fellow women and men, are prerequisites for oracle consultation. As an understanding of destiny, or God's personalized relationship with the individual is revealed, positive, sustainable growth and power are experienced.

Similarly, as individuals begin to walk their path of destiny, the power of peaceful, loving thoughts, emotions, and actions that reflect God's image and likeness are, also, experienced. To sustain connections to destiny, consciousness elevating meditations and rituals are most impactful for devotees. These rituals also endure connections to truth and purpose, while synchronizing, and aligning body and spirit to God, whose divine laws are displayed throughout nature. For Constantine and most of the contemporary Western and industrialized world, God's law reflected within the balance and harmony of nature is severely violated, as Earth's natural resources are decimated.

Chapter Eleven

Thousands of Years Before Christ: A Metaphysical Lifestyle Initiates Women and Men into an Ausarian (Osiris) Elevated Consciousness

The Arch of Constantine may represent a shallow prehistory framework, where one of the most elaborate and intricate spiritual-initiation systems existed in ancient Kemet (Egypt). Regarding a Christian syncretism, similarities among Christ, Mithras, and Krishna have been discussed. Remaining are conversations about the African, Heru, or Greco-Roman, Horus, predating Christ by thousands of years. Through spiritual invocation, in ancient Egypt or Kemet, people actualized and brought to life experiences and encounters with the angelic, liberating power of Heru (Horus), and the Black African, Ausar, or Greco-Roman, Osiris. Initiated common women and men, ceaselessly experienced peaceful and joyful lives, while actualizing and realizing Ausar (Osiris), or the consciousness of an internal, living god.

Comparing the socio-religious traditions of ancient Kemet (Egypt) with that of Mithraism and Christianity: motifs of god, Mithras, do not depict him as directly dying, then resurrecting from the dead. In literary analysis of socio-religious texts, Heru (Horus) is described as the son of, and resurrected incarnate of Ausar (Osiris), who is the father that died at the hands of his brother, Set. In contrast, Roman art and sculpture depict Mithras as grabbing an animal by the nostrils, which possibly symbolizes the rich, spiritual history and culture of Apis bull veneration of Kemet. The syncretism is that Mithras, who is described as the son, stabs the bull in the torso so that his father Osiris (the Europeanized Ausar) can be resurrected. Within this militarized society, Roman generals embodied the energies of Mithras, who often adorns the same regalia as elite officers. Mithras (Europeanized Heru) stabs the bull in the torso, spilling its blood, so that his father Osiris could be resurrected. Envisioning themselves as the virulent Mithras, Roman generals embarked on the world to colonize Eastern and Western provinces.

Within this historic, socio-religious syncretism, the ancient African and Egyptian (Kemetic) god Ausar is resurrected as a Greco-Roman and Europeanized, Osiris, due to the shedding of sacrificial blood onto a mound of soil. Between Mithraism and Christianity, the shared cannibalistic credo and visualization from sacrificial ritual that celebrates violence and bloodletting is the eating of flesh and drinking blood in remembrance of Mithras and Jesus. Quite possibly this socio-religious ritual is to perpetuate the cycle of violence that secures the privileged status of elites.

In a much broader sense, similar pagan rituals exist in animistic traditions, such as Black African Vodun, where animals are sacrificed then eaten. In certain animistic traditions, animal sacrifice and bloodletting are forms of divination, where devotees put into practice, harmonizing information received from the ancestral realm of spirits. For the acquisition of physical power and material possessions, it appears that Caucasians and Europeans desire the metaphysical, occult, and esoteric, spiritual insight of Africans. Truth be told, on their high-holy days, Abrahamic and monotheistic Jews and Muslims also perform animal sacrifice. The European lack of experience at cultivating peaceful thoughts and emotions, while in deep meditation and oneness with the occult, subconscious, and spiritual domain of Ausar, results in a lifestyle that nourishes the major, controlling emotion of fear. In spiritual matters, corruption and ineptitude often manifest themselves in physical and empirical deficits being expressed through war and genocide.

In the book, "*Egyptian Dawn: Exposing the Real Truth Behind Ancient Egypt,*" Robert Temple begins by referring to Ausar, or Osiris, the Greek name for this Kemetic Neter (deity, god, ancestor, interdimensional spirit being, facility of the spirit, and/or manifestation of nature). In specific chapters of his book, Mr. Temple focuses on the Tomb, or shaft of Osiris, where elaborate-initiation ceremonies took place. Thousands of years before Christ, and the Greco-Roman or European use of electricity, tombs were chiseled into solid bedrock at least 100-feet in the Earth. This may have been done with physical labor, but what lighting source illuminated the area as work progressed more deeply to form three tiers of subterranean caverns? Mr. Temple says the following about this possible replica of Osiris' (Ausar's) tomb, which is on the third level of the tunnel where a "... stone sarcophagus [weighing thousands of pounds] sits on an island surrounded by water, from which Osiris rose from the dead. This is meant to symbolize the site of his divine resurrection."

The tunnel leading to subterranean caverns is barely shoulder width. How did the ancients transport massive sarcophagi (coffins) through these tight caverns, and into confined niches? Possibly, unacknowledged psychic forces, or metaphysical technology were used to construct caverns, by leveraging the consciousness and spirit of initiates, who had attained the status of an Ausar (Osiris). Initiates who cultivated and lived a divine, spiritual, and metaphysical lifestyle became a resurrected Ausar during their lifetime of physical existence. Thousands of years before Greco-Romans, the resurrection of Christ, or the coronation of Flavius Constantine, African initiates engaged in elaborate, spiritual, and metaphysical ceremonies. In the ancient world, the title of Ausar was not limited to one individual, but was appended to the name of initiates, or common women and men, who diligently endeavored to elevate their consciousness and spirit to the highest levels. This is the meaning of life eternal: invoke or commune with ancestors through meditation, ceremony, and ritual, so that they can share ancient wisdom and teachings, through their avatar or incarnate.

In the Kemetic (ancient Egyptian) pantheon, Ausar is a divine and auspicious god, king. In contrast, his brother, Set, became consumed with jealousy and anger, due to Ausar's priestly relationship with common women and men. Set then conspired to usurp the throne by murdering his brother. Before the birth of Ausar's son, Heru (Horus), Set tricked his brother into lying in an enticing, golden sarcophagus. Set then closed the lid trapping his brother. With Ausar's body confined inside, the beautiful and intricately designed coffin was thrown into the Nile River. Auset (Isis), Ausar's sister and wife, later retrieved the burial chamber. Set seized the coffin and cut Ausar's body into 14 pieces and scattered them throughout the world.

Auset (Isis) devotedly searched the globe and retrieved 13 of the 14 pieces of the body. Sebek (Anubus) embalmed or mummified Ausar (Osiris), who through metaphysical means was resurrected from the dead. The phallus is the missing 14th piece, and through metaphysical means, Auset transfigured into the Ba, a human headed bird. The Ba of Auset carrying the shen ring in its talons, alights on Ausar's abdomen. This results in Auset becoming pregnant and later giving birth to Heru (Horus). Without known sources of electric lighting, initiates portrayed and reenacted Ausar's resurrection from the sarcophagus in The Tomb of Osiris: chiseled out of solid bedrock, with a pristine water flow representing the Nile River.

The three central Neteru, gods, or deities of the Ausarian (Osiris) tradition are different from the trinity of Christianity, represented by the father, son, and holy spirit. The central Neteru represent a more approachable and accessible forms of divinity within the family unit: Ausar is the father, Auset is the mother, and Heru is the son. Possible ambiguities concerning Abrahamic traditions, and specifically Christianity are that the father is The Creator Being, who initiated the formation of all things, approximately 13.9 billion-years-ago. In contrast, the father, Ausar of Black African, Kemetic traditions is not described as The Creator Being. However, 2,052 years ago, with the coincidental, triumphant rise of the Roman empire, this same Creator Being, father, is now a Caucasian male who through immaculate conception, a human virgin is impregnated to give birth to a son. Conventional, scientific evidence proves that 13.9 billion-years-ago a Caucasian male was not the cause of an explosion to create an expanding universe of galaxies, solar systems, and planets with life forms.

Here is an irrationality based on lacking evidence yet employed to support incorrect beliefs: Approximately, 2,052 years ago this omnipresent, omnipotent, and omniscient Creator Being impregnated a human female. The direct hand of God, or an unknown, yet to be experienced body part proceeded to intervene resulting in the birth of a son, who is the savior of mankind (Homo sapien sapiens), in existence for at least 250,000 years. While inflicting war atrocities on pigmented people, who occupy resource-rich territories, Greco-Romans celebrate egotistical materialism, and redefine religion and spirituality to reflect their hypocritical lifestyle of genocide and self-service. To reshape Greco-Romans as god and savior of humankind, their socio-religious and educational institutions rationalize hegemonic, warmongering behavior as natural and acceptable.

The following questions remain: Why did the son of God, or Christ, come into being to only save humankind, given that the father gave birth to an entire universe 13.9 billion-years-ago? Approximately 2,021 years ago, at his death and resurrection, why did the son of God leave behind his holy spirit, which was already in existence with the creation of the universe 13.9 billion-years-ago? In 325 CE, these questions and concerns were debated at the Council of Nicaea, from which Biblical canon emerged. The Nicene Creed is another doctrine of control that emerged from the council, intended to standardize a religious oligarchy of Roman Catholic manipulation and patriarchy.

Alternatively, a conventional, scientific explanation of creation might say that 13.9 billion-years-ago, before there was physical matter, a singularity of compressed consciousness exploded releasing energy, or spirit to form the universe. An eclectic description and approach to conventional science might converge with creationists' understanding to declare that all things emanate from God. A creationistic version of the laws of conservation of energy, matter, and consciousness might also assert that everything returns to God to be recycled. In a similar light, practitioners of metaphysical science use meditation to focus and co-mingle their consciousness and spirit with that of God to access Its creative power, thus enabling practitioners to transform thought and emotional energy into physical matter. Meditation, and other forms of esoteric science allow practitioners to connect their divinity to that of God's. Trance induction, meditation, and other metaphysical practices assist initiates, also, engaged in a life of study to know that consciousness is the guiding principle that directs energy flow, or spirit, to transition subatomic particles (quarks, bosons, gluons, etc.) into physical matter.

Through initiation, common women and men begin to identify with a lifestyle that exemplifies the Neteru, or angelic possibilities and ancestral veneration. In Ausarianism, images, statues, and other forms of art depicting family: the mother, father, and children can be held as sacred. More inclusive, holistic, and approachable forms of divinity are also practiced, in the sense that common women and men are not deliberately limited and confined to low spiritual levels, but are initiated and encouraged to rise above their animal nature to become an avatar, experiencing and living as a Neter (Ausar).

Resurrection and Rebirth of the Divine Self: Ausar

To embrace an understanding of spiritual science is to apply practices to slow the rate of thoughts entering awareness, so that the conscience, or indwelling voice of God can be listened to and followed. Practitioners who engage in diligent spiritual practices can also activate communication engendering relationships with the Neteru, or higher states of God's consciousness to influence positive change in the world. Changes occur as devotees study and practice techniques to harmonize internal-spiritual power or electromagnetic, bioelectric, and biochemical flow of energy, which becomes enhanced to coincide with planetary, cosmic, and universal consciousness. Study and application of spiritual practices in real-world, practical situations now become a functional life-science that reunites devotees with God. Practitioners then become a force for good, inseparable from The Creator. Contrary to contemporary, deceptive indoctrination for mass control, this is the true function and intent of religion: liberating people through spiritual unification with a loving and beneficent God. The experience of divine unification is rooted in love, as opposed to fear.

The attributes and qualities of the father (Ausar) are similar to those of Hinduism's Krishna. The exemplary talents of the godhead are represented through the unifying ability to access

God's omnipresent attributes through Its shared consciousness, dwelling in all things. Deep meditation techniques and trance induction refine this talent to commune with God's consciousness. In ancient spiritual cultures of prehistory most people exemplified the Neteru, or gods' positive qualities. Within a hierarchical social structure, however, it is one king or queen, who was the godhead. Generally, in the contemporary era, practitioners begin to know that all things are interconnected and interrelated through experiences and relationships with this omnipresent and primordial, universal consciousness.

Similar to kings, queens, other royalty, and common people of antiquity, contemporary practitioners of spiritual science begin to express qualities of Ausar, or Krishna. Practitioners emulate the divine attributes and talents of a Neter, deity, or god during their Earthly sojourn. This is a more accessible model of divinity: practitioners study to emulate the specific, positive attributes and spiritual energies of the gods, or Neteru. Practitioners also strive to cultivate the personal attributes or personality of a Neter, god, or ancestor to become their embodiment, or avatar. After experiencing this impactful, insightful, and liberating life experience, most devotees are reluctant to relinquish this cultivated expression of divinity. This is evolution: spiritual practices are maintained to inhibit returning to an existence consumed by the materialistic trappings of the lower-human, or animal nature.

Practitioners can emulate the devotional quality of the Black African Neter, Auset, (European Isis). The terms devotee and devotion are similar in that they both connotate a sincere commitment to a positive, spiritual lifestyle. Auset (Isis) was so devoted to her husband, brother, and king that she searched the globe to find the 14 pieces of Ausar's body. An innate feminine ability incubates the mother's devotion and sincerity to bring life into the world. This physical process of nurturing and supporting life can also symbolize the spiritual growth, development, and power foundational to cultivating Auset's energies. Without her devotion to find the 14 pieces, Ausar's body could not be reassembled, resurrected, and reborn.

A possible conclusion is that devotion to esoteric, occult practices are successful attempts at assembling into a conclusive and definitive whole, the parts of both the physical and the spirit body, otherwise known as the Chi, kundalini, or Ra. In a much broader sense, this holistic process can also indicate effective communication with The Creator, or indwelling conscience to bring practitioners closer to their divinity and self-realization. Devotion to attaining divinity enhances one's physical and spiritual wellbeing. Performing meditative rituals to tie the physical and energy body back to God develops talents and abilities that can be recognized as forms of rebirth: Shedding the old person, who is easily influenced by materialist societies. Shedding the old person also permits a transition into the ever existent, and eternal-divine self. Initiates begin the shift into spiritual adulthood, by relinquishing childish and adolescent, materialistic, egotistical, and fearful behaviors of the lower-human, or animal. These physical, empirical, and noticeable acts of purification and change are similar to the symbolic resurrection of Ausar, or the indwelling, divine self.

However, this rebirth cannot effectively take place if initiates have ulterior motives, or are insincere, and corruptible – ulterior motives in the sense that they desire to use spiritual power solely for self-dealing, self-serving gratification, and acquiring material possessions. This internal conflict between initiates and their indwelling God manifests in a divided body, or one who is severed physically and is spiritually disjointed due to moral turpitude, which inhibits rebirth, and the resurrection of Ausar.

Chapter Twelve

Divinity is The Will to Choose to Make Correct, Conscious Decisions

In a more generalized and symbolic sense, as some people begin to spiritually grow, mature, and evolve, they may accept and realize that true happiness is not attained from the acquisition and accumulation of material possessions. True happiness, less affected by Maya or empirical illusion, is the eternal peace and joy acquired from sharing with and helping others. This shift from the severed, but healing and mummified body of Ausar, who is resurrected and reborn, can also represent the cyclic, daily, rising and setting of the Sun. After nightly rejuvenation and instruction from the inner planes of sleep and dreams, every day, daughters and sons of God are reborn to fulfill the positive legacy of The Creator's work here on Earth. Even conventional science has proven that negative mental and spiritual consequences can result from severed connections to the inner planes. For example, prolonged sleep and dream deprivation can result in insanity. Understand the relevance of work initiates perform to maintain connections to God. By stilling thoughts to listen to and follow the conscience, or subtle communication from an indwelling God, initiates also strive to acquire talents to release the self-centered, corruptible ego.

A major quality of Auset, and Ausar's son, Heru (Horus of the Greco-Romans), is the will, or the right and ability to choose. Throughout this text, the evidence driven, codifying message has been that modern humans are being deceived, misdirected, and miseducated about their origin and purpose in life. This ensures that the species perpetually serves, worships, and is the physical or mental slave to profit-driven corporations, and institutionalized forms of government. Within this environment that is infiltrated with, and directed by Maya or empirical deception, it is challenging for the masses to implement their true, or divine will, which stems from an omnipresent and omnipotent God. Practicing humility as well as rhythmic, esoteric breathing during meditation to slow the flow of thoughts entering awareness are possible prerequisites to connect with divinity and God's will.

To interfere with direct two-way communication with God, instead of peace, quiet, and stillness, contemporary societies often promote busy mental chatter, media noise, and distractions as acceptable forms of illusion. To hear directly from God, traditional oracle systems such as the Kemetic Metu Neter, and Chinese I Ching can be employed, in conjunction with meditation. However, to integrate God's will into their lives, diviners must humbly forgive themselves, as well as others for real, or contrived wrongdoing. Humility and receptivity to follow God's will also has a positive impact on nature, and the lives of others.

The added challenge to implement divine will stems from widespread socio-religious dogma, superstition, and ignorance that demonizes pigmented people, whose occult rituals provide greater access to God, and the supernatural. Moreover, demon and devil worshipper labels are attempts to vilify a diasporic, traditional-African lifestyle, where mediumistic trance and other divination techniques are practiced. Remaining in the contemporary era are the residual, negative effects of psycho-spiritual and physical terror, at the hands of slaveholding societies. Therefore, diasporic Africans use ancient, spiritual traditions and mediumistic trance to heal from subtle memories of atrocities that manifest as symptoms of post-traumatic slave experiences encoded in their collective consciousness and DNA.

By the 1860s, in all the US: military, government, and civilian agencies carried out targeted acts of systematic terror to subdue over 6 million African people, 33% of the Southern population, held in perpetual chattel-slave servitude. Associate Professor of African American History at Emory University, Leslie M. Harris, suggests in her book "*In the Shadow of Slavery*" that few Northern industries illegally enslaved Africans, forcing them to toil in factories that processed raw materials from the agricultural south. Slaveholding societies, mortified by the very thought of rebellion and insurrection, used generational terror to subdue captives. To secure hegemonic dominance, these societies enforced, through terror, the notion that African ancestors are demons and ritualizing with them is demonic. This is, or was, to obstruct and inhibit the intergenerational flow of ancestral energies to achieve spiritual evolution and physical liberation.

Causes of Distortion that Inhibit Lifestyle Choices Aligned to God's Will: Heru Faculty

Continuing the conversation about Heru (Horus), or the will and the right to choose, a brief comparison of modern and ancient societies may be appropriate. In most contemporary industrialized societies, modern humans or Homo sapien sapiens are accepted as the highest, or most physically evolved form of life, primarily due to their dexterity, and intellectual prowess to design tool-making technology. From antediluvian prehistory, where societies chose to develop and employ technologies to cultivate positive-spiritual traditions and divinity to connect the species to God's natural love and mercy, the shift has been to this current, pervasive consortium of war machines. In this current display and definition of civilization, nations touting aggressive forms of religious, socio-economic, or governmental ethics tend to dominate those who lack military defenses and strategy. Modernization and corruption have become defense mechanisms to protect nations against occupation and mental subjugation, at the expense of psycho-spiritual initiation systems that cultivate liberation, love, and freedom to commune with God's universal consciousness.

Other than rationalizing the design and advancement of war technology as forms of progress, modern societies also celebrate analytical thinking and intellectual prowess, which can condone and support negative behaviors that contradict spiritual growth and evolution. This intellectual ability to choose to rationalize negative emotions and behavior, distances mankind from higher forms of spiritually evolved life, nature, and God Itself. Not accepted as a disciple by Western academia, but on higher levels of spiritual science, it is understood that rationalization of negative behavior nurtures a conflicted internal environment, similar to the symbolic, severed body of Ausar. Learning from ancient Kemetic traditions, this fractured body of mankind needs physical, spiritual, psychic cleansing and purification for healing. Historically, socio-religious cultures such as African, Native American and Australian, Eastern Hinduism, and Buddhism that practice arousal of innate extrasensory, or psychic and spiritual faculties to advance to higher levels of evolution, have been attacked and decimated through imperialistic war institutions.

Prior to forced assimilation into monotheistic, Abrahamic belief systems that function behind the veil of empirical and religious elitism, there was violence to deter and decimate ancient traditions that cultivate practices to arouse extrasensory abilities, and psychic perception. Mass enlightenment and spiritual liberation are elitists' greatest fear, because it results in a self-controlled citizenry, adhering to the internal voice of God. Most threatening to elitism is a mass citizenry not driven and controlled by mindless consumerism. Instead, citizens would make determined and deliberate economic choices, which do not support the corporate, fascist agenda of elitists' control. Given these contemporary societies that rationalize negative emotionalism resulting in imperialism, war, and mass control, people can still choose to align their will, or Heru faculty to divinity and destiny to make correct choices, leading to a life that is positive and purposeful.

Well Informed Thorough Research to Positively Impact the Heru Faculty: The Will and the Freedom to Choose

To develop strategies and reasonable answers to cultivate Heru and make choices in life that synchronize with God's will, consider the conventional term, dog whistle, to describe racist rhetoric and policies, such as Black Identity Extremists, and wars on drugs, terror, and immigration. Also, consider government infiltration and counterintelligence programs, such as cointelpro from the late 1950s, throughout the 60s, and into the early 1970s. Cointelpro intends to maneuver people into key organizational positions in programs and movements to instigate assassination of pivotal African American leadership. Released official FBI documents refer to surveillance and infiltration tactics, possibly designed to result in the murders of Malcolm X (1965), the Black Panther Party's Fred Hampton and Mark Clark (1968), as well as Martin Luther King (1968).

Bear in mind that Africans of the diaspora cannot fully assimilate into demented global Western societies, since Black people will not be accepted, and are the continual target of White supremacy. The foundation of Eurocentric society is constructed on a patriarchal platform of White-identity politics and racial purity and supremacy. These ideologies and practices are laughable considering the Caucasian propensity to copulate with African slaves. Using Caucasian pejorative jargon, race mixing (miscegenation) produces a defiled bloodline of tainted, lighter-skinned mullatos, destined to the caste of house negros Consider the renowned relationship between slaveholding, American-founding father, Thomas

Jefferson, and his slave, Sally Hemings, which produced a bloodline of further racial impurity. Clearly, political disinformation that supports and insulates White-identity politics and power relationships are conflicted and irrational, since it is based in emotionalism. In very simple terms, regardless of dignity and the rights of others, feelings of superiority continue to reward and nourish the selfish and self-centered ego. In a 2019 interview, frenzied supporters of demagogic President Trump admit to his gaslighting, and their loyalty to him is based on feel-good emotions. Their statements are similar to the following: "President Trump just makes me feel good to be White again."

Africans on the continent and throughout the diaspora need not function out of feel-good emotions, since this results in further control by demagogic ruling elites. In the arena of spiritual evolution, a fulfilling lifestyle may require petition of higher, angelic lifeforms and ancestors to impact an outcome of positive change. Positive ancestors and angelic lifeforms repel and retract from the fear, hatred, and deceit that is seminal and inspirational to White nationalism and identity politics. Historically and spiritually, African people should admit to, and accept their uniqueness. Information is external, but historic evidence, such as the election and accomplishments of America's Black president, Barack Obama, is an exemplar of African uniqueness, regarding rational-political thought and forward momentum. To have a positive impact, correct and insightful information should be internalized, ritualized, and celebrated to become truth applied in real-world situations, thereby optimizing Heru actualization to yield beneficial results.

Global populations should accept that the role and purpose of conventional, institutionalized government is not to bring mass populations to a place of spiritual liberation, enlightenment, and self-awareness. Instead, government subtly promotes through mass-media propaganda that spiritual, angelic enlightenment of higher forms of life and existence will result in anarchy, through violent riots to overthrow the established order. To the contrary, throughout 2020, not because of an overt higher calling, but in global protests against police brutality and systemic racial inequality, the *Black Lives Matter Movement* has sparked the flames of institutional reform. This progression toward change indicates a more conscious and aware citizenry, who have awakened their Heru (Christ) faculty. As an affront to mindless consumerism, the flames of boycott have been actively rekindled against financially supporting an amoral, corporate-elitists' system of mental and psychic control.

In the affirmative, the entire species and planet are on the path of spiritual enlightenment. Consider the shift in energy consumption from climate change causing fossil fuels, compared with Elon Musk's, Tesla electric car technology, solar panels, and SpaceX rocket innovations. Mr. Musk has other projects and an agenda to grapple with the inevitable rise of the machines, (AI) Artificial Intelligence. To mitigate AI's existential threat to mankind, he has launched a tech startup company, Neuralink, that designs electronic implants to connect the human brain with a computer interface via artificial intelligence. A July 2020, internet article by Natashah Hitti states:

> The approaching technology would see groups of minuscule, flexible electrode "threads" implanted into the human brain by a neurosurgical robot. These threads detect and record the electrical signals in the brain, and transmit this information outside the body. This has the potential to create a scalable high-bandwidth brain-machine interface (BMI) system, meaning that it connects the brain to an external device to form a brain-machine interface. The goal is to use Neuralink to understand and treat different forms of brain or spine-related disorders. For instance, paralyzed humans could use the implanted device to control phones or computers. However, Musk also envisions the implant as a means of enhancing your own brain, giving humans the option to achieve a symbiosis with AI. This could eventually lead to a future of "superhuman intelligence", according to Musk. As he explained at the Neuralink Launch Event in San Francisco on 16 July, the idea is to create a "well-aligned future" that mitigates the supposed existential threat of AI.

Interfacing with AI technology could possibly result in superhuman cognitive ability. Not being explicitly considered, however, is that machines having wireless access to human thoughts may possibly allow AI to hijack the psyche by implanting ideas, images, and memories that are exclusively beneficial to AI advancement. Neuralink could also develop into an additional resource to bolster mass control by shaping a reality that holds human mental ability captive within a prism of AI control. In this alternate reality, AI may become the puppet masters instead of the current ruling, established politicians and other elitists.

Even with limited and less certificated use of AI technology, as proposed by author Dr. Judy Wood, a fear-driven reality is fomented that blames Muslim terrorists for using an energy weapon to dustified (turned to dust) The World Trade Center. Other than AI, there is the more heinous side of socio-political and economic conservatism, where the status quo is maintained by elites wielding weapons of mass destruction, while exploiting Earth's natural resources.

Chapter Thirteen

Societies that Promote Detachment from the Neteru (Nature) and God's Divine laws

It is possible to actualize aspects of the Heru faculty through heightened awareness of history, along with current events to understand that public and private institutions hold the planet, and species in a physical and mental-time bubble that upholds and supports the controlling, conservative power of elitism. For example, educational systems continue to rationalize and promote as acceptable the subtler practices of eugenics, scientific racism, and social Darwinism. These practices and philosophies are encoded into the educational fabric and framework of societies that promote racist theories, such as Charles Darwin's strict evolution, touted in: "*The Descent of Man,*" published in 1871.

Couched and conveniently nestled within strict evolutionary theory are false notions that indigenous Africans and Australians evolved directly from primates, but Europeans and

Caucasians are civilized and far removed from Black people, and nature. In his 1871 publication, Mr. Darwin asserts:

> At some future period, not very distant as measured by centuries, the civilized races of man will almost certainly exterminate and replace throughout the world the savage races. At the same time the anthropomorphous apes, as Professor Schaaffhausen has remarked, will no doubt be exterminated. The break will then be rendered wider, for it will intervene between man in a more civilized state as we may hope, than the Caucasian and some ape as low as a baboon, instead of as at present between the negro or Australian and the gorilla.

Seemingly, Charles Darwin, as well as those with a similar imperialistic, political, and socio-economic worldview are inclined to define a *civilized state* as being able to decimate nature, while carrying out genocidal atrocities against pigmented people: the *anthropomorphous apes.* Clearly, Mr. Darwin is saying that African people are a subspecies of human. In a more generalized sense, all pigmented people, lacking Caucasian characteristics and phenotype are a subspecies. Based on this genocidal paradigm from 1871, the European *civilized state* condones, promotes, and rationalizes rape, murder, and other atrocities.

As modern and forward thinking as the imperialistic mindset and worldview considers itself to be, its radical strict-evolutionary theory of modern human origin and purpose stems from the incestuous Darwin and Wedgewood bloodline. At the age of 29, the man celebrated in textbooks as the father of evolution, Charles Darwin, proposed to his first cousin, Emma Wedgwood, the daughter of his mother's brother. Mr. Darwin and his wife Emma had 10 children. Three of their offspring died before age 10, two of them from infectious diseases. Although in long-term marriages, three of the six surviving children did not produce any offspring. This suggests to contemporary researchers that Mr. Darwin's incestuous marriage affected reproduction in his lineage.

Ignorance and a lack of clarifying language also becomes evident as those of Abrahamic belief begin to place into discussion the rather simplistic statement that they do not believe in evolution. The conventional, scientific-fossil record proves that physical evolution does occur. Everything, animate and inanimate, slowly changes overtime, which ancient-pigmented people know to be true. On one hand, Abrahamic belief ostracizes ancient narratives and traditions of pigmented people as pagan and demonic, yet, metaphoric explanations of divine human origin are foundational to all theistic systems of knowledge, monotheism, polytheism, and animism. Contradicting divine origin, the theory of strict evolution is most controversial and divisive, since it claims that modern humans, specifically savage Africans and Native Australians, evolved directly from gorillas and baboons, but Caucasians are far removed and are in a *civilized state* of being.

This theory of strict evolution infers that humans are animals and there are no angelic beings, or higher forms of life in the universe, who have transcended this animalistic state of existence. Strict evolutionists also promote that Earth is the only planet in the universe where evolution occurs to support life. In favor of corporate and elitists' control, these theories and philosophies are woven into the educational fabric, so that students are taught and conditioned to identify with their less spiritually evolved animal. Miseducation about modern human origin and life purpose functions to form social and psychological programming that reinforces the idea that Homo sapien sapiens are directly descended from lower animals, who are in an emotional state, where self-control is lacking. As such, the government must intervene to control humankind through corrupt politics, White supremacists' policing, and a Black majority prison population.

To support an elitist military and intelligence-industrial-complex of mass control, people are also conditioned through nationalists' propaganda to join the armed forces. Even religion has become a corrupt mechanism of control through the ministry and message of prosperity: Bless the church and Pastor with monetary contributions and God will, in turn, bless the congregation with good health, and even greater monetary rewards. In contrast to the unsustainable and nonsensical systems of elitists' geopolitical, corporate, and religious control, purify and cultivate the Hrit chakra, or biological-psychic center, which is the same as the Heru faculty or the divine will and freedom to choose, to see past the veil of national, imperialistic deception.

In the contemporary era, European and Caucasian conservatism and elitism are more implicit, and takes the form of planned parenthood in American public schools, specifically targeting Black communities and sterilization programs in Africa, under the guise of immunization. These eugenic, population control programs are unnecessary, due to the current extinction event from Earth's magnetic pole shift and weakening electromagnetic field.

Speaks for Itself and Stands on Its Own: Rudyard Kipling's Poetry

Celebrate African ancestry and difference by accepting that irrespective of educational norms and socio-religious indoctrination, God's natural laws exist, as reflected in nature. To begin in 1845, but mentioned in ascending chronological order, specific racist philosophies were intentionally integrated into global-educational norms and curricula. Without proper descriptive explanation and clarification, but intended to sanitize and make justifiable crimes against humankind and nature, specific terms and actions similar to manifest destiny (1845), have been spun into the educational fabric. To highlight patterns of systematic decimation of nature and pigmented people living a positive-spiritual lifestyle, next is the racist philosophy of social Darwinism (1877), which also rationalizes human atrocity. The audacious dishonesty of social Darwinism also implies that genocide and extinction of nature, reflects natural law, embedded within nature itself. In other words, nature is designed to exterminate itself, similar to humankind carrying out genocide. Additionally, in reference to the absurd concept of the White Man's burden (1899), subtly promoted in academic textbooks are explanations to justify colonialism and imperialism. Rudyard Kipling, the author of the poem, *"The White Man's Burden,"* writes a most offensive stanza, which says the following about pigmented people:

Take up the White Man's burden—
Send forth the best ye breed—
Go, bind your sons to exile
To serve your captives' need;

To wait, in heavy harness,
On fluttered folk and wild—
Your new-caught sullen peoples,
Half devil and half child.

To be liberated from the negative words of Charles Darwin and Rudyard Kipling, as well as the racist, government institutions supporting White supremacists' action referring to pigmented people as captured animals, having traits from *Half devil and half child*, take into meditation images of a hawk, Heru, flying above its prey of miseducation. This hawk is aware of all that occurs, including nuanced, negative conditioning stemming from White supremacy. To cultivate the Heru faculty for mental, and psychic liberation from an inherently racist society, purify and stimulate the Hrit chakra, through the use of hekau (mantras and sounds of power) during ritualized meditation. In place of racist, educational indoctrination: Celebrate African ancestry and heritage.

Nowhere in nature is intellectual prowess to design weapons to carryout genocide and extinction of its own species considered natural. No other organism on Earth rationalizes war and destruction as being natural and beneficial progress. The implicit, but nefarious underlying reasons for war and destruction are greed, phenotypic or physical diversity, coupled with psycho-spiritual and evolutionary differences. Those with advanced war technology also tend to decimate, rob, and criminalize those with high-spiritual culture and civilization. Similarly, the human intellect rationalizes contradictory and conflicted behavior against its own wellbeing to the extent that it has coined the phrase manifest destiny (1845), to promote as divine an edict that justifies criminal behavior against Native Americans. Both social Darwinism

(1877) and manifest destiny support genocide based on phenotypic and spiritual evolutionary characteristics, such as ancient, ancestral rituals that cultivate talents to commune with nature, as an avatar for higher forms of angelic life.

Imperialism makes genocide and spiritual decimation more effortless and protracted, forcing native-pigmented people to convert, and assimilate into Abrahamic traditions that demonize African, Native American and Australian traditions and ancestry. Hypothetically, an unabashed, but honest, Abrahamic apologist would say: Convert and default to the position of military and socio-religious dominance to perpetuate genocide of demonic, indigenous people. This practice of demonizing others is aligned with Abrahamic elitists' belief in God's chosen people and is an indication of a childish, immature, and a self-serving understanding of The Supreme Being and divinity.

Heru: An Ancestral Understanding of the Freedom to Choose to be Always Peaceful and Joyful

To awaken the powers of Heru, the freedom to choose to live in balance and accordance with God's natural, loving laws as reflected within nature, might also mean becoming aware of historic narratives that aggrandize elitists military conquerors, and politicized global leadership. To bolster mass control, the media often depicts self-serving and materialistic leadership as happy, because of physical wealth and material possessions. Resulting control in the form of increased willingness to follow these media personalities is often a consequence of subtle and sublime messages through imagery, which encourages mass populations to emulate the self-serving and aggressive behaviors of business and geopolitical leadership. Again, the message is since these people have worked arduously to acquire the rewards of physical wealth, the masses should do the same, so that they can also be happy and blissful. This system of illusion also rationalizes misguided and greedy behavior as acceptable, modern, and trendy since this paradigm dominates the world. In simple terms, assimilate self-serving behavior to be outwardly happy, and accepted as normal.

In the contemporary era, to fulfil a lifestyle that reflects the ability to choose inner-eternal peace, which may stem from memory activation of ancestral greatness, might also require a community to assist with cultivating positive thoughts, emotions, and actions resulting in spiritual empowerment. Community and support are most essential to encourage fulfilling a positive, spiritual lifestyle. For this reason, engage in research to find the best fit that accommodates individual, as well as community needs. Specific spiritual societies teach meditation techniques to effectuate the continuous experience of instant gratification from always being peaceful, resulting in joy and eternal happiness. This is the effect of the practitioner's will and consciousness influencing the spirit to realize and accentuate a symbolic Heru and Ausar in real-time, on this physical plane of existence.

This positive-spiritual lifestyle also models balance and harmony in nature. An additional expectation of this peaceful, self-actualization is mitigating and transcending the previous effects of practicing delayed gratification, which tend to inhibit expressions and experiences of joy, before accomplishing mundane, worldly success. In other words, the celebration occurs when the goal or project is completed. Celebration of life, itself, should be continual throughout the project, as well as at its completion. Heru is the freedom to choose to transcend emotional impulses, while always being peaceful and joyful (happy) through sharing physical possessions and love. These behaviors are connected to fulfilling altruistic goals and desires, while not harming others or the environment, and not placing personal health in jeopardy.

Another major, but controversial aspect of implementing Heru, or the freedom to choose to live in accordance with God's divine, natural law is knowing the conventional scientific, as well as spiritual reality that matter, energy, and consciousness are neither created, nor destroyed. Those who practice and know creationism might say that matter, energy, and consciousness return to God, The Creator of all things to be recycled. In quantum physics, the *Double-Slit Experiment* illustrates the subtle influence of consciousness, as it affects energy to shape matter formed on the subatomic level. This experiment demonstrates that consciousness, or conscious, focused intent, while in the waking state (Heru), has an effect on energy (spirit).

For example, when the observer is not focused on the *Double-Slit* apparatus, energy behaves as it normally would: It goes through the slits in the lead plate, while interacting with itself to form a distortion wave, or interference pattern on the other side of a solid lead barrier. However, when a conscious observer of the experiment is present, energy flow begins to function similar to matter. Energy still goes through the slits, but in this instance, there is no interaction of particles or distortion wave pattern. This may be because the observer perceives physical reality, and expects the particles to go through the slits, without interacting with each other, in the same manner that matter functions. On the other side of the double slit, there is no distortion pattern, indicating that the particles did not interact with each other. This experiment demonstrates the ability of consciousness and will, while in the waking state (Heru) to influence spirit, or energy to create, and manifest physical matter on the subatomic level of particles.

Comparatively speaking, DNA is physical matter because of its consistent molecular structure, however spiritual energy has metaphysical properties, as well, given its less-dense arrangement of subatomic particles. Both DNA, and the spirit or Qi body stores information and memories. As mentioned previously, simple conventional scientific research shows that birds hatched, and raised in captivity, still remember the intricacies of nest building. This information is stored in inherited DNA. On the metaphysical level, the spirit or Qi body also stores information and memories, as discussed by the honorable Dr. Ra Un Nefer Amen, author of the *Metu Neter* series.

A sort of symbiotic relationship exists where DNA and the spirit or Qi body conveys symbiont information, possibly transcending time and space, to become life-affirming knowledge having a positive impact on the contemporary host-vehicle. One caveat: Be mindful that information and memories stored in DNA are not confined or limited to one previous life or incarnation. During semiconservative DNA replication and cell division: meiosis and mitosis, memories stored in genetic information, can span multiple generations and millennia. In this model of DNA replication, each new strand contains information from the original template, or parent strands that are thousands of years old. Quite possibly, the genetic blueprint of DNA is universal, and shared throughout the cosmos. This concept of interplanetary DNA may be evident in Brien Foerster's research of the fossilized Paracus skulls, a type of Homo capensis.

Ancestral spirit energies having past-life memories can integrate into physical bodies, but are not limited to one specific DNA lineage or bloodline. The invocation of positive or negative ancestral-spirit energies and memories are more dependent on the devotee's lifestyle. Cultivate negative thoughts, emotions, and actions, then the physical vehicle becomes a receptacle or repository for cosmic-negative energies and memories from the past or future. If a person's life was filled with negative, ignorant influences and no positive-spiritual lessons were learned or retained, there is no forward momentum or upliftment from the initial, childlike state of incarnation. Regardless of material wealth, levels of education, or other mundane successes, some adults never mature past the spiritual and emotional stage of adolescence. They remain confined to spiritual stagnation.

These interactions among spirit energy, DNA, and the physical body provides a viable causeway through which essential cosmic, ancestral information and knowledge can be transferred and inherited by current generations. For those who are inclined to be more atheistic, but still interested and curious about past-life regression hypnotherapy, research Delores Cannon. These truths concerning the eternal nature of spiritual existence dwarfs limited perceptions of race, class, or socio-religious denomination.

Chapter Fourteen

African Civilizations are the Oldest and Most Spiritually Evolved

Daily meditations to awaken Heru, or the slumbering Christ within are also rituals that might integrate Qi Gong, Yoga, and oracle divination systems to cultivate positive, behavior changing experiences that can assist with transitioning the incarnate, or initiate to higher levels of spiritual development. These ritualistic behaviors result in a renewed understanding of the ancient meaning of life eternal. Simply put, the cycle of eternal life becomes more evident as initiates begin to heighten their awareness through metaphysical practices. Positive spiritual initiation makes more seamless, the possibility of choosing to forgo the mistakes of past lives, as memories and experiences from previous incarnations are stitched into everyday reality. Memories of ancestral, metaphysical, and megalithic accomplishments are also awakened from within the DNA of contemporary initiates, as they travel to, and relive spiritual experiences, messages, and teaching from the inner planes, or the everlasting and eternal. These forms of African ritual fulfillment are what those of the Abrahamic tradition would call near-death experiences. For Africans, it is death to the lower-emotional animal, who fearfully, or faithfully holds on to material possessions and hurtful experiences that impede spiritual liberation and oneness with God.

Moreover, the uninitiated masses are conditioned to refute and disregard the realities of cultural diffusion, as evident through the son, Heru, being an incarnate of his father Ausar. This spiritual tradition and lifestyle preexisted Jesus, who is supposed to be an incarnate of the father, God, Itself. Seemingly aware of cultural diffusion, however, Robert Temple in his book "*Egyptian Dawn: Exposing the Real Truth Behind Ancient Egypt*" compares the life of Christ to that of Ausar (Osiris) and Heru (Horus). In the following statement, Mr. Temple makes a brief comparison of Jesus and Ausar: "Like Jesus, according to the Egyptian myth, Osiris died, was buried in a tomb and rose from the dead. And also like the Christians story, the open and empty tomb itself symbolized the resurrection that had taken place."

Mr. Temple does not say directly, but alludes to Christianity borrowing from the prehistoric, antediluvian-knowledge system of Ausarianism. Chronologically speaking, Kemetic (ancient Egyptian) civilization predates Persian and European societies. Evidence of this is torrential-rain erosion on the Great Sphinx of Giza in its current desert environment. This geological evidence dates the megalith Sphinx to at least 9,000 years in the past. This age of 9,000 years is much older than the 5,000-year date given to Sumer, in Mesopotamia, the first civilization defined in history textbooks.

Most contemporary, uninitiated Christians would not accept historical evidence, which ties their traditions and belief system to that of Mithras, or to basic occult and metaphysical practices, such as prayer and meditation to awaken Heru, or Christ within. Similarly, those of Abrahamic traditions have a superficial and shallow understanding of incarnation as it relates to expressing ancestral memories stored in inherited DNA. Depending on the positive or negative lifestyle of initiates or host-vehicle, aligned and associated spiritual energies take up residences in these physical bodies. These natural phenomena exemplify the impactful significance of Heru (Christ), or the will to choose to live in accordance with divine law, as reflected within nature, so that negativity is challenged to find internal domicile. Indoctrinated with incorrect belief, the uninitiated masses are taught to fear the occult, since interaction with it results in demon possession. Based on spiritual teachings, however, considered as demonic are negative thoughts, and emotions that result in corrupt behavior, such as deliberate failure to confront habitual greed, and determined inability to share material possessions.

To rationalize negative behavior, historic narratives from high-ranking officials may reference the Pope, or previous Roman Emperors as Christ incarnate. This is so that mass followers can worship socio-religious and political, elitist leaders. In the past, if subjects of elitist leadership did not follow religious doctrine and dogma, the European Inquisition (1300s through 1800s) labeled dissidents as heretics, which was a reason to inflict physical and psycho-spiritual torture. Followers of Christ were also kept under control through the belief and mindset that dissension against incarnated nobility and priesthood would incur suffering in the pit of hell, for eternity. These actions, philosophies, and teachings contradict an all loving and merciful God. Why would an omnipresent, omnipotent, and omniscient mother God cause Its creations to suffer for eternity in the fire of hell? Additionally, the masses are controlled through ignorance and misguided beliefs, promoting a segregated heaven with isolated sections for members of each of the three-Abrahamic faiths, and everyone else is destined to burn in hell for eternity. Another subtle, but existential conflict for believers is Christ's humble, meager lifestyle, and spiritual teachings are not modeled or emulated throughout the generations of opulent-Roman Emperors, Papal priests, and Protestant ministers.

The Shaft of Ausar (Osiris): The Father of Heru (Horus)

Stark differences exist when discussing the actual, ancient Egyptian (Kemetic) tombs, where mummified remains could be excavated, compared with the unverified empty burial chamber of Christ Jesus. In Kemet, mummified remains stayed undisturbed for thousands of years, and visibly signal use of advanced technology to craft solid stone into sarcophagi, weighing forty tons. These sarcophagi are unearthed in numerous locations throughout the ancient world, and are harder than the iron or copper chisels, thought to be tools of that era. Unlike the single, unverifiable empty tomb of Christ, on numerous occasions vacant, megalithic sarcophagi are revealed throughout Kemet, not only in the King's Chamber of the Great Pyramid, but also in the Serapeum of Saqqara, along with the tomb or Shaft of Osiris (Ausar), located beneath the stone causeway of the Pyramid of Khafre.

Here is the contradiction, however, when celebrating ancient Kemetic, psycho-spiritual and socio-religious culture and traditions, compared with a Roman-crucified corpse in Abrahamic Christianity. Living initiates, such as priestesses and priests, as well as royalty used these ritual sarcophagi during ceremonies to become an Ausar, by reenacting his resurrection. This ritualized act of resurrection is contrasted by Abrahamic Christianity, where exclusively a corpse is laid to rest in the tomb. For them, pious consumption of transubstantiated flesh and blood causes an experience of mental and spiritual transformation into a docile, Christlike resurrection of Greco-Roman mass control.

Seemingly in support of Abrahamic Christendom, Mr. Temple also says the following: "Christian tradition is full of references to 'the empty tomb' and it forms the subject of some hymns. It is specifically mentioned in the four canonical gospels. The empty tomb is thus central to the entire message of Christianity."

Christian narratives also commemorate an empty tomb as evidence that God triumphantly healed and resurrected Jesus, after he was scourged, crucified, and the final death blade thrusted into his side by a Roman centurion. This literal socio-religious event celebrating a physical death and resurrection is unverifiable through historical and conventional scientific research, but this Christian narrative can be contrasted by the more ancient traditions of Kemet. Here, ritualized ceremony can include a tomb and sarcophagus (coffin) shaped out of stone with metaphysical properties to help living initiates elevate their consciousness, through trance induction and reenactment of Ausar's resurrection.

In terms of ancient, holistic, and spiritual practices, which today are misrepresented as superstition, Mr. Temple verifies that these sarcophagi were the craftsmanship of Kemetic people, due to its location in Africa. He also questions the historic opinion that rope and pulley technology were used to lower forty-ton stone sarcophagi down the Shaft of Osiris (Ausar), to be later placed into three levels of subterrain niches:

> The sarcophagi bear no inscriptions or carving of any kind, and are thus completely plain. How these huge, weighty objects were lowered by rope and kept steady is a challenge to the imagination. What were the chances of such things swinging against the sides of the shafts, bashing the sides (there are no traces of this) or being dented or scratched themselves (there is no trace of this either)? How were they steadied and how were they lowered? We do know that the ancient Egyptians had stone pulleys for raising and lowering extremely heavy weights by the Fourth Dynasty at least.

The spiritual practices of ancient Kemetic, megalithic society and culture allowed access to metaphysical technology, not attainable today, but is described by some as superstition. Possibly, to gain access to the metaphysical realm, while in a deep meditative state, ritual and symbolism speak to the spirit of initiates as they lie in the sarcophagus, during ceremony, to reawaken with the elevated consciousness of an Ausar. A positive, spiritual lifestyle is not superstition, but coincides with beneficence and dedication to humility, to deserve the title of an Ausar, appended to the name of initiates. This is the relevance of ritual, ceremony, initiation, and divinity for Kemetic, African people.

In an attempt to interpret, then communicate ideas about ancient Kemetic artifacts and lifestyle, Mr. Temple continues to reference the Shaft of Osiris (Ausar):

> At this second level, one is confronted with a substantial chamber containing seven niches, and in the northeast corner a further opening leading down to a third level. The level which until recent years was flooded. The descent into that third level is by a leaning ladder, about thirty more feet down. In Level Two of the Osiris Shaft, the seven niches, evidently burial niches, are arrayed along the south, west and north walls of the chamber, with none on the east. As we have seen, in 1944 there were sarcophagi in all of them, but only two of those were large. The place had been so hopelessly plundered since 1944, with all but the largest sarcophagi having been taken away (unrecorded, to unknown destinations, apparently).

Comparatively speaking, by today's Westernized, materialistic standards, it is challenging to understand and emulate the alternate, spiritual lifestyle and reality of Kemetic people. They spent extensive hours in meditative trance, while breathing rhythmically, and chanting mantras or hekau to commune with ancestors, higher angelic beings, and the forces of nature. This meditative process also stimulates psychic centers or chakras to elevate consciousness to access talents, such as precognition, clairvoyance, telepathy, and telekinesis. In dominant contemporary societies, foreign to

Abrahamic socio-religious tradition is upliftment of consciousness through positive-spiritual initiation, ritualized with oration and symbolism, along with rhythmic drumming and dance to speak to the spirit. The practice of cultivating positive spirituality for liberation through consciousness elevation is not exclusive to incarnates, who possess the holy spirit of the only begotten son of God, but is an inclusive and holistic lifestyle, accessible to everyone.

To preserve mummified remains, Mr. Temple says that in the Shaft of Osiris (Ausar), radioactive granite and basalt were crafted into sarcophagi that also killed bacteria. His extensive research into the mummification process permits him to know that, except for the heart, internal organs were removed and placed in canopic jars, representing the four sons of Heru. Then the body was packed with natron salt for forty days to remove all moisture. Desiccation killed or decayed all bacteria, thereby preventing the need to irradiate the mummy. If living initiates participated in ritualized ceremonies, by lying in sarcophagi to symbolize death to the less spiritually evolved, lower-human animal, there would be no need to irradiate a mummy. Perhaps, the beneficial purpose of this ceremony was initiates raising, resurrecting, and being reborn with the elevated consciousness of an Ausar. The radioactive properties of the stone sarcophagus may have served another unexplained purpose, perhaps assisting initiates through consciousness elevation. Mr. Temple also suggests that radiation levels caused priestesses and priests to develop leukemia, or white blood cell cancer, within twenty years or so, since they worked long hours to craft the sarcophagi. This is supposition on his part, since he would be unaware of herbal medicines, or other remedies the ancients used to mitigate the effects of radiation. Mr. Temple says the following:

> Something which seems never to have been realized by Egyptologists before is that sarcophagi made of granite, basalt and related stones are so powerfully radioactive that a corpse placed inside would be so intensely irradiated that – like the irradiated food sold in supermarkets – it would have extra 'shelf-life', and most of all of the decay bacteria in the mummy would have been killed off. . .. I suggested taking these readings because of our findings in the Valley Temple, where the granite was so amazingly radioactive that we decided that any priests or attendants working there regularly would have contracted leukemia or some other form of terminal cancer . . .. These radioactivity issues seem to be a new finding, as neither of us has ever heard or read of such matters being mentioned before by anyone.

Compared to contemporary empirical and materialistic societies, Kemetic people existed and lived within a metaphysical, positive-spiritual reality inundated with symbolism and ritual to manifest enriching, meaningful experiences of divinity. Because of this, Kemetic holistic science is enigmatic and incomprehensible, when defined and compared by using the same metric as dominant, Westernized philosophical thought and action. When discussing his research into the type of mysterious stone used to craft Sarcophagus Two, Mr. Temple seems baffled: "We were later to discover by mineralogical X-ray diffraction analysis what [type of rock Sarcophagus Two] really was, and this would give us a shock." Laboratory reports came back saying that it was a stone called dacite, which globally is a limited resource, and no natural vein exists to produce the extremely large Sarcophagus Two. On consultation of books on Egyptian geology, Mr. Temple discovered that:

> . . . the only dacite deposits I could find mentioned were in the far Eastern Desert and the Sinai, which are hundreds of miles away from Giza, with no convenient route for transportation of large stones (the far Eastern Desert is beside the Red Sea and not beside the Nile, and the Sinai is on the other side of the Red Sea). Jules Barthoux, who wrote about these occurrences of dacite in those out-of-the-way places, mentioned that dacite mostly exists as veins running through other rock. Extracting a solid block for a sarcophagus from such a vein is all the more problematic and bizarre, as most of the veins are not large enough to enable such a feat to be physically possible. These veins are sometimes vertical, making access and extraction particularly difficult. When Barthoux found a piece of dacite from a vein that was approximately 1.5 meters thick, he seemed to think it was unusually large and splendid. But even that vein was not nearly large enough to produce the huge dacite sarcophagus in the Osiris Shaft. It seems that dacite is not a common Egyptian rock by any means, and it was never used for any of the tens of thousands of small stone vessels roughly contemporary with the sarcophagus. In fact, there appears to be no known occurrence of its use in any ancient Egyptian artifact or construction, other than for carving this enormous Sarcophagus Two in the Osiris Shaft.

Chapter Fifteen

Deceptive Machinations and Concoctions of the Mind for Mass Control

As evidence of Jesus' resurrection, the empty tomb described in the Gospel of Mark provides a rather simplistic rendition that conveniently introduces Joseph of Arimathea. For implying that he is the son of God, Jesus is found guilty of blasphemy, by the Sanhedrin council of which the never before mentioned Joseph of Arimathea was a member. Compared to contemporary judiciaries, the court system in Judaea was expeditious, considering that the territory was in turmoil with Roman occupiers battling rebellious, Hebrew residents. Under such violent conditions, a backlog of seditious criminals awaiting sentencing would be expected.

Seemingly, within hours or a few days, the Sanhedrin council and King Herod remanded and adjudicated the political prisoner, Jesus. In the end, Pontius Pilate, the Roman governor of_Judaea under Emperor Tiberius condemned Jesus to death. After the rapid final verdict, he is first scourged, then crucified on the Friday before Passover, one of the holiest days of the Jewish calendar. Bear in mind that the entire Sanhedrin council condemned Jesus to death. The Gospel of Mark directly says that council member, Joseph of Arimathea went to Pontius Pilate to request Jesus' body. In so doing, Joseph was in defiance of his very own council. Given this traditional Abrahamic context, Mark's Gospel implies that by going to Pilate, Joseph risked Sanhedrin ridicule, and jeopardized his aristocratic prominence and stature.

Nonetheless, Pilate granted Joseph's request to have Jesus' body. According to Jewish tradition, it was taboo for a Sanhedrin to defile himself by handling a corpse, on the day before Passover. Through some unexplained miraculous feat of human strength, by himself, Joseph carried, then climbed a ladder, and dirtied his fine clothes to remove nails driven into Jesus' hands and feet. To carry the deceased to the tomb, Joseph further bloodied himself, while wrapping the stabbed and scourged corpse in a linen shroud. He then draped the body over his shoulder, taking it to the tomb, where he rolled away a huge stone blocking the entrance.

The Gospel of Mark continues – Mary Magdalene and another woman named Mary observed Joseph retrieving Jesus' body and placing it in a tomb. Bart Ehrman, professor at Chapel Hill University, and author of "*How Jesus Became God*" says that these events set the stage for the discovery of an empty tomb and are essential pillars for the resurrection and ascension narrative. On the day after Passover Sabbath, Mary Magdalene and two other women went to the tomb, but found it empty. Christians say that the resurrection of the only begotten son of God, who rose on the third day is a literal event, but simple arithmetic contradicts this doctrine. The first 24 hours after Friday's crucifixion is Saturday. Two days, or 48 hours from Friday is Easter (Ishtar, Isis), or resurrection Sunday for Christians. Mr. Ehrman continues by saying that "If there were no tomb for Jesus, or if no one knew where the tomb was, the bodily resurrection could not be proclaimed. You have to have a known tomb."

Mark's Gospel was written after Paul's epistles, but his letters reveal nothing about Joseph of Arimathea, the respected Sanhedrin according to Mr. Ehrman. He references Paul's creed in I Corinthians as an oath that begins to establish a structural framework for organized Christian *beliefs*. The term socio-religious *belief* system is acceptable to Abrahamics. However, *beliefs* represent an uncertainty that may be correct or incorrect, since they are not based in fact and evidence. Mr. Ehrman's analysis spotlights contradictions of logic and reason, since prior to Mark's Gospel, Joseph of Arimathea is not mentioned. Comparing the Gospel of Mark with the earlier epistles of Paul, one disparity is that Paul's epistle mentions Caphas as the person to whom Jesus appeared after his crucifixion. Other than in a *belief* system, chronological sequencing would dictate that Paul mention Joseph of Arimathea placing Jesus' body in a tomb, before describing Caphas' encounter. Mr Ehrman says the following:

> . . . if the author of that creed had known such a thing, he surely would have included it, since without naming the person who buried Jesus, as we have seen, [Paul] created an imbalance with the second portion of the creed where he does name the person to whom Jesus appeared

(Caphas). Thus, this early creed knows nothing about Joseph. And Paul also betrays no knowledge of him.

Unlike the Gospels (Matthew, Mark, Luke, and John) biographical narratives about the life of Jesus, the book of Acts was written by an unknown author, referred to as Luke, who researched older writings to formulate his compilation. Luke is also said to be a Greek physician, but it is noteworthy that he proselytized about Jesus more than sixty-years after his crucifixion. Scribing these narratives sixty-years after the fact makes Luke's writing secondary or tertiary sources of evidence. Mr. Ehrman says that "Scholars have long recognized that Luke himself wrote the speeches . . ." in the book of Acts. Most contemporary laypeople are unaware of this historic writing style, which makes the speeches in Acts bogus, since it falsely represents the words of apostles Peter and Paul, who apparently risked their lives proselytizing the Gospel throughout the Roman empire.

The Gospels themselves admit that the majority of Jesus' apostles were fishermen. At the time, most fishermen lacked formal education. A logical conclusion is that most apostles were also illiterate. It stands to reason that illiterate apostles were incapable of documenting the life of Jesus. Other than this, historians and scholars know that Luke's writings appeared decades after the supposed historic events of Jesus. As referenced by Mr. Ehrman: "the ancient Greek scholar, Thucydides, in his writings about the Peloponnesian War 1.22.1-2, says it was common practice for historians to compose speeches for their main characters." In the case of the book of Acts, the scribe is referred to as Luke, and his characters are the apostles Peter and Paul.

In Acts 13, the author referred to as Luke writes about the apostle Paul speaking in a synagogue in Antioch of Pisidia (modern day Turkey), where he preached about the Jewish council's transgression against God – the conspiracy to put Jesus to death. Historically, the council of Jews were not executioners, who performed the gruesome task of crucifixion, nor did the Sanhedrin have the authority to sentence anyone to death in Roman held territories. In his writing, Luke creates the theory that the Sanhedrin persuaded or inveigled Pilate to have Jesus put to death. Luke writes further that in this synagogue, Paul's sermon vilified the Jewish Sanhedrin, since they found no charges deserving of death. Instead of acquittal, the Sanhedrin passed the case to Pontius Pilate's higher court for sentencing.

It appears that Paul, the former Jew, infiltrated the synagogue at Antioch, in attempts to convert rebellious Hebrews to accept the more pacifistic teachings of Christ. In an effort to migrate Jews to pacificity, Luke writes that the Sanhedrin act of inciting Jesus' death was prophetic – foretold in Hebrew indoctrination and scripture. The confusing inconsistencies in these Christian narratives are that Mark's gospel mentions Joseph of Arimathea, but Paul's epistles show no evidence of Joseph's existence, but mentions Caphas, instead. Now Paul, in the book of Acts, says that the entire Sanhedrin council removed Jesus from the cross, and placed his body in a tomb.

Scholarly, historical engagement with New Testament narratives about Jesus' burial and resurrection begs the question – was his body placed in a tomb? To substantiate a resurrection, there has to be an empty tomb. For ancient scribes attempting to organize a socio-religious institution, with the influence and support from Roman state sponsors, perhaps the enduring issue became how to weave this empty tomb narrative into existing doctrine? There are possibilities, but can they be properly scaffolded into a believable and plausible history? One solution is to weave edited renditions into existing texts about Jesus' crucifixion, where people closest to him removed the body from the cross, then placed it into an empty tomb. Jesus' family is eliminated, since they were of lowly stature and had no access or means to acquire a burial chamber. Another possibility is to have Jesus' followers or disciples place the body in a tomb, but they fled the scene in fear for their lives. Remaining is a high-ranking Jewish official, or the entire Sanhedrin council. As mentioned previously, one person, Joseph of Arimathea, removing and burying the corpse is an implausible, Herculean task, still included in Mark's Gospel. Most acceptable is that the entire Sanhedrin council removed the body. As Mr, Ehrman says: "And so that is the oldest tradition we have, as in Act 13:29. Possibly this is the tradition that lies behind 1 Corinthians 15:4 as well: and he was buried."

Truth Verified by History: Live Divinity as the Daughters and Sons of God

In order to make it seem as though Jesus' divinity sparked a glimmer of hope in certain people, by speaking to their indwelling conscience, the Gospel of John mentions Nicodemus accompanying Joseph of Arimathea to remove the corpse, and placing it in a tomb. Joseph of Arimathea appearing to be influenced by Jesus' divinity, causes him to become a secret admirer, and possible follower of the

Messiah. Then there is Pontius Pilate, who hastily condemns Jesus to death in Mark's Gospel. By Matthew's Gospel, however, Jesus' divinity seemingly begins to affect Pilate who becomes more reluctant to sentence him to death. In both Gospels of Luke and John, there is greater internal deliberation as Pilate has a soliloquy with his conscience. During this same inquisition, on three separate occasions, Pilate declares Jesus' innocence, until prodded by the Sanhedrin to issue the death sentence. Mr. Ehrman says: "In later Gospels from outside of the New Testament, Pilate is portrayed as an increasingly innocent good guy, to the point that he actually converts and becomes a believer in Jesus." Clearly, there is Roman biased influence in scribing and compiling New Testament scriptures, since the texts increasingly exonerates and makes Pilate an innocent bystander. However, the apparently unredeemable Jews conspired to put to death a fellow Hebrew, who conveniently became the Christian Messiah.

In Israel, at the time of Jesus, Roman authorities were the administrators of secular law and policy enforced by its military. Christian apologists often insist that Jesus' corpse had to be removed from the cross on Good Friday, since the next day was Passover, a high-holy day in Jewish socio-religious custom. Historical records affirm that Jews did not have state control in Israel. In addition, non-Jewish, militaristic Romans were not inclined to respect Hebrew sensitivities aligned to burial law and tradition, especially for a condemned criminal, charged with sedition. To maintain fascists' control through established Roman law and order, and as a deterrent to insurrection, criminals were physically tortured and left to die and rot on the cross, as public spectacles. Not allowing criminals a decent burial, but having them decompose on the cross was a form of humiliation in this life, as well as the next, since socio-religious burial rights assist the deceased with spiritual passage into the hereafter.

All too often, conveniently forgotten is that according to Biblical narratives, both authoritarian Roman and Jewish elites: The Sanhedrin council, and Pontius Pilate found Jesus guilty of seditious crimes against the state. Jesus did not confess to committing blasphemy, but simply agreed with the Sanhedrin, who placed him on trial for being a son of God. Jesus' crime was that of being a spiritual figurehead, who criticized the contrived Jewish moral conscience that overflowed with elitists' hypocritical practices: using temples for fee-based currency exchange, as well as a market for sacrificial animals. Jesus' sedition was that he preached and mobilized against the corruption and hypocrisy, supported by both Jewish and Roman established elites, who wanted to maintain their place of worship as materialistic gods. For dispelling patrons and toppling tables in the temple, Jesus, a rebellious change agent against the established Jewish and Roman order, was put to death by crucifixion. Ironically, Jews are in search of a Messiah, but not a spiritual personality such as Jesus. For Jews, their Messiah is not one to condemn Hebrews for hypocritical practices, but is a militaristic, socio-political and religious leader, who would physically liberate Israel from Roman occupation.

Mr. Ehrman's historical analysis of the life of Jesus goes even further by saying that "John Dominic Crossan has made the rather infamous suggestion that Jesus' body was not raised from the dead but was eaten by dogs. When I first heard this suggestion, I was no longer a Christian and so not religiously outraged, but I did think it was excessive and sensationalist." However, there is historical evidence in support of the Roman practice of having crucified criminals remain on the cross to be eaten by wild animals. There is an ancient inscription found on the tombstone of a man who was murdered by his slave in the city of Caria, which says that the murderer was "hung . . . alive for the wild beasts and bird of prey." The Roman author Horace also said in one of his letters that a slave was claiming to have done nothing wrong, to which his master replied, "You shall not therefore feed the carrion crows on the cross" (*Epistle* 1.16.46-48). There was also the Roman satirist Juvenal who spoke of "the vulture [that] hurries from the dead cattle and dogs and corpses, to bring some of the carrion to her offspring" (*Satires* 14.77-78).

Chapter Sixteen

Mental and Spiritual Liberation are not Found by Assimilation into Societies that Promote Sycophantic Acceptance

All modern humans (Homo sapien sapiens) are on the path to enlightenment, whether they are aware, or not. Those of the Abrahamic socio-religious tradition also have psychic experiences of incarnation and destiny, which reach beyond the confine of empirical reality and the five senses. These shared experiences may take the form of Deja vu, premonitions, or clairvoyant dreams and visions. Comparing ancient civilizations of high culture to that which currently exists, consider the downward-spiritual spiral from following aggressive, dominant socio-religious and governmental systems that control through fear. Mass-media and church sermons project fearful words, and imagery of terror attack and eternal damnation in hell fire. These are methods of control through psychic, mental terror: mass populations are programmed and indoctrinated by repetitive words, negative imagery, and symbolism which causes excessive fearful thoughts, and emotions of suffering the punitive consequences of burning in hell for eternity.

Recall scenes of bloodletting from Mithraic temples that have been syncretized into symbolic cannibalism, or ritualized transubstantiation acted out by contemporary Roman Catholic priests, Protestant ministers, and their congregation. Assessment of these symbols, and messages presented through religious iconography suggests that mass populations should partake in ritualized sacrifices that subtly celebrate the routine torture of others. For example, there is the slaughter of the Mithraic bull, and the crucifixion of Jesus, often referred to as the sacrificial Lamb of God. This frightful and controlling imagery permits the Greco-Roman establishment to send a message that bloodletting and violence are acceptable means to exterminate dissent and defiance. Other than bloodletting, socio-religious indoctrination also contends that the souls of those who do not follow the Abrahamic, or Christian order, will burn in hell for eternity. Exposure to these forms of psycho-spiritual and socio-religious indoctrination, along with conditioning through imagery, and actual physical violence, programs the species to rationalize and accept as normal, atrocities committed against each other, as well as nature.

In response to fear-driven Abrahamic sermons, parishioners and congregants begin to conjure up imaginary, emotional experiences of burning in hell for eternity, which negatively impacts the spirit, thereby confining the soul, and psyche to an empirical reality. For mass control, instead of liberation and healing, words (spells) are used to weave imagery that bind, limit, and confines the spirit to a fear-driven reality. Certain recurring religious iconography, imagery, and teachings specific to the torturous crucifixion of Jesus, also, generates empathetic experiences that embeds fear into the human psyche to cause a downward-spiritual spiral and devolution.

Words are stitched together to form imagery and symbols that speak to the spirit, to further inhibit deeper, positive-psychic visions from past incarnations and destiny. In simple terms, fear is the stopgap for positive, spiritual, psychic experiences and evolution. In addition, so-called modern Abrahamic, socio-religious institutions do not encourage the study and practice of ancient paradigms to correctly interpret and explain positive-spiritual experiences, such as Déjà vu, and premonitions. Instead, they label the ancients as demons, infidels, and goy who interbred with fallen angels to produce a hybrid species. These xenophobic, misguided philosophies and doctrines promote fear, ignorance, and superstition. Liberation from this act of mental and psychic control requires studying spiritual cultures of prehistory and their ancient societies, as well as practicing meditation techniques to awaken Heru, or the freedom to choose to hear from an internal God, who guides all creation to live in peace and harmony.

Abrahamic Lifestyle of the Sycophant: Inhibition of Mass Mental and Spiritual Liberation

Discussions comparing the historic significance, as well as the names of archetypal personalities, such as Mithras, Krishna, Heru (Horus), and Christ Jesus demonstrate syncretistic relationships between religious and spiritual traditions. In this text, Roman traditions venerating Mithras that tie closely to pre-Christian history and iconography of sacrificial bloodletting have been emphasized. In Mithraism, the central motif of animal sacrifice is the blood of a bull emptied onto a mound of soil, resulting in the rebirth of Black, African Ausar as Caucasian Osiris. In this imagery, Ausar rises from the soil as an incarnate and embodiment of a Greco-Roman, or Caucasian god. Similarities between a dying and resurrecting god are, also, briefly alluded to in the mythos and mystic qualities of Ausar, and Christ Jesus.

Other socio-religious and syncretic relationships between Mithras and Ausar result in extensive discussion of Heru (Horus), the son of Ausar. In the ancient Egyptian (Kemetic) spiritual tradition, Heru is a symbolic representation of Homo sapien sapiens' evolutionary stage where, throughout the day, while in the waking state, the will is accentuated to co-mingle with the spirit to carryout correct, or incorrect voluntary action. Along similar lines of incorrect behavior, Western or Greco-Roman civilization uses socio-religious institutions to perform transubstantiation rituals to project crucifixion imagery and narratives, which secure hegemonic power, as they implement policies and technology to further mass control. This hypocritical, socio-religious behavior is in direct opposition to offering spiritual and mental, mass liberation. Throughout history, central to mass control is empire formation, such as with Flavius Constantine convening the Council of Nicaea to organize a Roman Catholic church to further entrench military and political power.

Compared to periods of mass illiteracy throughout the Roman empire under Flavius Constantine, the contemporary era has vastly improved rates of literary comprehension. However, most members of Abrahamic traditions use simplistic and childlike analysis to critique sacred texts. As New Testament scholar and professor, Bart Ehrman, of Chapel Hill University, North Carolina says: "Christian literature is read vertically, the same as a novel, instead of horizontally for scholarly analysis and comparison." If laypeople were to use scholarly analysis of the different Gospel characters, chapters, and narratives, they may draw factual conclusions about Abrahamic-sacred texts. This sensible critique is contrary to Abrahamic traditions that emphasize adherence to sacred texts and its concomitant rituals, as forms of indoctrination and mass control.

To hinder inquiry into deceptive practices by Abrahamic scribes and other literate elites, researching the origin and intent of specific psycho-spiritual rituals, such as animal sacrifice and burnt offerings is highly promoted as taboo. Still practiced in the contemporary era is bloodletting and animal sacrifice during Abrahamic high-holy rituals. Historically speaking, these rituals originate with the first people, African priestesses and priests from pagan, non-monotheistic traditions. However, as Abrahamic monotheists gained influence and power to enslave Africans, they labeled the original priestesses and priests as pagan-devil worshippers and demons.

The previous historical consideration of African people may be viewed as falsehood, since in dominant, Abrahamic traditions, mass populations are socialized into sycophants, who indiscriminately follow socio-religious and geopolitical leadership without questioning. Sycophantic attitudes and behavior do not result in spiritual and mental liberation. However, it may stem from nuanced memories, and remnants of force assimilation through terror and fear tactics, still encoded in inherited DNA. This, in turn, generates a need or desire for acceptance by members of dominant societies, who continue to promote mass control through crucifixion iconography, and other Abrahamic practices of sacrificial blood offering and ceremony. In the contemporary era, certain monotheistic traditions, such as Protestant Christianity tend to project grisly symbolism as they say: *The unredeemed, as well as children in Christ, must be washed in the sacrificial blood of Jesus, for salvation.*

Chapter Seventeen

In the Beginning There Was Consciousness

As an extension of this trend to control others through psycho-spiritual manipulation, at the 325 CE Council of Nicaea, both Bishops Alexander and Arius continued to deliberate and hold firm to differing socio-religious ideologies. Both Bishops were in positions of leadership in Alexandria, and their presence is evidence that prominent, religious philosophy emerged from the Eastern empire of North Africa, specifically Egypt (Kemet). This also suggests that the foundation of Christian and Abrahamic philosophy preexisted in regions of Africa. Furthermore, as esteemed ecumenical councilmen serving in Egypt, a former Greco-Persian or Ptolemaic stronghold, Bishops Alexander and Arius were privy to Coptic or first Christian church literature and teachings from approximately 42 CE. These Coptic teachings may have assisted with shaping the Bishops' burgeoning, Christian ideology and rhetoric. Metaphorically speaking, as experts in Christian theology, Alexander and Arius (of Libya) may have served as gatekeepers, drinking from the reservoir that nourishes, and sprang forth similar ideas about creation and the fall of humankind, for whom a divine Christ was sacrificed to bring salvation.

Alexander and Arius are also described as subordinationists, firmly holding on to the idea that a divine Christ: the only begotten son of God, was sacrificially crucified as part of his Father's plan for salvation of humankind. The term, subordinationist, describes a theologian who holds the following concept as sacred: The son, Jesus Christ, is subordinate to The Father, God, The Creator of all things. In a more conventional sense, in the beginning, 13.9 billion-years-ago, there was an explosion from which sound, as well as God's consciousness and spirit were emitted, culminating in the creation of an expanding universe. Moving forward in time, past the original explosion from which the essence of all things came in existence, there is the awesome sound of God's power as heard through nature, such as the crash of tumbling ocean waves and thunder, along with the wolf-like howl of hurricane wind.

Seemingly, there lacks understanding that at creation of an expanding universe, God was not speaking words. Neither were there people, 13.9 billion-years-ago, who could interpret the sounds of God, within nature, as being understandable and discernable words. Prior to Christianity, however, the Serapis Christus cult made famous by Ptolemy I, also refers to *the word*, which is later translated into Latin to signify logos. Other than being subordinationist, theologians go further by saying that logos can, also, strictly refer to the inner thoughts of God, expressed outwardly in words and other communication. The most pressing questions remain: Who or what can qualify to understand the awesome thoughts of God, The Creator of all things? Does God express Itself through thoughts and words? Nonetheless, Alexander and Arius steadfastly held firm to the Christian, Latin (Greco-Roman), or Ptolemaic concept of logos.

Again, along the lines of sycophantic indoctrination, the idea of logos is also written into the New Testament where it says: *In the beginning was the word, and the word was with God, and the word was God. The same was in the beginning with God. All things were made by Him.* In the Abrahamic-patriarchal tradition, God is male, and this explains the statement: *All things were made by Him.* However, in the older socio-religious tradition of pigmented people, the female is a more accurate expression of God, since it is she who internally nurtures, then brings life into the world, the same as The Creator Being. There are also African languages, similar to Metu Neter, that speak the awesome sound of God as heard and represented through nature, the Neteru, and ancestors.

Pigmented people have an older, more holistic, personal understanding of an all good and loving, creator God. Being made in the image and likeness of an all beneficent and loving God, traditional people know divinity by continually purifying their minds, so that God and the ancestors can inhabit the body to share positive, life affirming experiences. This positive, spiritual lifestyle contradicts Abrahamic traditions, where proselytization is emphasized to bring others into the fold, so that they can be controlled by manipulative elitists.

The Nicene Creed: A Solution to the Arius Controversy at the 325 CE Council of Nicaea

While discussing a main Bishop who was present at the council of Nicaea, Dr. Mary Cunningham, Professor of Religious Studies at North Carolina State University says: in primary-source letters, Arius does refer to Jesus as the son of God. According to the Abrahamic-Christian tradition, this title of the son of God is the same as the logos, and the word. Arius, however, did not accept that Christ is coeternal, with God. What he meant by not being coeternal, or not of the same substance as God (Heteroousios), is that Jesus is on a level of divinity that is greater than creation. In other words, Christ's spirit or essence was in existence with God before the creation of everything else. Most importantly, however, it is God who is eternal, and was in existence before Christ. Arius' Heteroousios doctrine was later adopted by the Eastern Orthodox Church of Byzantium. According to Dr. Cunningham, based on the writings of Arius, Jesus seems to be in an intermediate region of divinity, since he is the first entity to exist with God, before the creation of everything else.

At the 325 CE Council of Nicaea, a much larger group of theologians agreed with the teaching and philosophy of Bishop Alexander, however. This group comprised strict originists, Bishops holding firm to the concept that the logos, Christ, is coeternal with God and is continuously generated by Him. According to originists' doctrine: the father always had a son, who is the logos and the word. They also teach that Jesus is of the same substance as God and is homoousios. Originists emphasize that it is Jesus who is made in the expressed image and likeness of God. As such, Christ is fully God and existed, or still exists, eternally with the father.

As the dominant majority, the originists gained support through Emperor Constantine, as they deliberated and conceptualized the meaning of the Holy Trinity and Christ's divinity. Emperor Constantine was not a theologian. His primary purpose for convening this ecumenical council was to consolidate his socio-religious, military, and political power. As the originists conceptualized The Holy Trinity, a Christian, or Roman Catholic oath referred to as the Nicene Creed then followed. The influence of Bishop Alexander and the originists is crystallized within a single sentence from the Nicene Creed: *We believe in one Lord, Jesus Christ, the only Son of God, eternally begotten of the Father, God from God, Light from Light, true God from true God, begotten, not made, of one Being with the Father.* Interestingly, this sentence from the Creed begins with *we believe.* The Nicene Creed as a pillar of Roman Catholicism and Christianity contains socio-religious indoctrination that is founded on *belief*, which may be correct or incorrect. In contrast to knowledge, Abrahamic religion and Christianity are founded on *belief*, instead of accepted, corroborated, historical, scientific fact and evidence. This form of socio-religious indoctrination, such as pledging an oath of *belief*, may be misleading parishioners, conditioned through hegemony and state-sponsored terrorism to be mindless sycophants, aimlessly following leadership masquerading as Christ incarnate.

As evidence that Roman Catholics and Christians have experiences of incarnation, recall that Eusebius Pamphilus, Emperor Constantine's official biographer, became convinced that Constantine was Christ incarnate, while Pamphilus was revising the emperor's biography to include visions, and signs at the Milvian Bridge. The phrase in hoc signo vinces: In this sign you shall conquer is most memorable as Pamphilus envisions Christ's spirit incarnating into Constantine's body, so that Maxentius could be defeated at the Milvian Bridge. To accept the notion of elitism, in terms of Emperors, Popes, and Priests being God's chosen few, the experience of incarnation is also written into the Nicene Creed, as it says: *For us and for our salvation he came down from heaven: by the power of the Holy Spirit, he became incarnate from the Virgin Mary, and was made man.* This oath implies that to be obedient adherents to Christ, parishioners and congregants must follow Emperors, Popes and Priests, who are Jesus' representatives and incarnate of the holy spirit, here on Earth.

Chapter Eighteen

Eurocentric Spiritual Evolution: Methodologies to Incarnate Christ's Holy Spirit

Written into the biography of Emperor Constantine, along with the Nicene Creed is a belief, understanding or experience of incarnation. The Nicene Creed speaks about: *by the power of the Holy Spirit he (Jesus) became incarnate from the Virgin Mary, and was made man.* In order to maintain control, elitists' leadership makes it appear that they are the chosen, exclusive incarnate of Christ's holy spirit. If the process to cultivate talents to incarnate Christ's spirit were understood and taught as a spiritual science, instead of being some sort of mysterious, secretive endeavor, the information would be shared. Are those who claim to be under the influence, or in possession of the holy spirit, simply not charlatans? This is a sensible question based on the elusive and cliquish nature of those who claim to be incarnates. They may be in possession of a spirit, but how does the congregation know for certain that it is the one and only holy spirit? Herein lies the dilemma, spirituality is not taught as a scientific practice with instructions on how to cultivate metaphysical talents. In Abrahamic Catholicism and Christendom, consumption of the holy eucharist (body and blood of Jesus) is supposed to cause a form of transformation, wherein the holy spirit alights or mounts the parishioner. This mass, ritual, or celebration purports to allow congregants to partake in a shared experience of Christ's incarnation.

Although Abrahamic, socio-religious texts and indoctrination are referred to as spiritual, there is no formalized, step-by-step guidance to cultivate and share abilities to liberate the spirit beyond the physical five senses. Excluding Catholics and other Christians, the ritualistic consumption of the holy eucharist can be considered superstition, since for most clergy and congregants, a contrite, Christlike life of piety is also deficient. After Flavius Constantine, Roman Catholic Emperors, Bishops, Popes, and Priests have been historic warmongers, in the name of Christ Jesus. These religious leaders of the institutionalized Roman Catholic church also invested in, and gained tremendous wealth from the Black, African chattel-slave holocaust (1500s to 1800s). During WWII, from 1939 to 1945, some Catholics in religious leadership also declared allegiance to Nazis, Mussolini, and the Axis forces. Throughout these hypocritical secular and religious policies there is a deliberate lack of shared spiritual experiences of self-actualization and empowerment as articulated by congregants' clarifying language. From the pulpit, parishioners do not receive clear expectations and guidance to induce positive, spiritual experiences before or after consuming Christ's body and blood.

Study of Roman history and empire reveals that Emperor Constantine convened and organized Catholicism and Christianity into a state sponsored religion. In general, this brand of religion was organized by people, who today would be considered as Greco-Roman and Caucasian. Instead of being holistic, the practice of this version of spirituality is segregative and isolationist. For a few hours, on one day of the week, humankind's ability to evolve into divinity seems to be the central focus. After the redemptive event of purification that may involve consumption of the holy eucharists, adherents return to business as usual. Again, and again, parishioners return during the following weeks and months to pay homage for the possibility of redemption and purification. This seems like a never-ending cycle of seeking forgiveness for wrong behaviors.

When does humankind gain access to methodologies for self-empowerment that enables use of specific, consciousness elevating tools and practices that deter wrong behavior? As individuals experience spiritual liberation through the redemptive qualities of self-control, and meditation with divine imagery and chants of hekau (sounds of power) to purify the lower chakras, wrong thoughts are emptied and no longer followed by inappropriate actions. Purification empties the person of inappropriate thoughts and emotions, and that void can be then filled with positive-spiritual images and behaviors that are Godly and divine.

In contrast, spiritual practices solely for gain of material possessions are hypocritical and insincere, to say the least. Misguided and conflicted congregants who may be purely seeking material gain through spiritual empowerment are also taught to circumvent accountability to themselves and their indwelling God, by repeatedly seeking forgiveness for selfish behavior. Seeking forgiveness without a sincere willingness to love and beneficently share material possessions, does not result in changed behaviors that reflect the image and likeness of a God that limitlessly gives and shares of itself. The deceptive and misguided practice of aimlessly seeking forgiveness, possibly results from ecumenical teachings that are deficient in appropriate symbolism, terminology and language that distinguishes divinity, positive spirituality, and love from that which is secular and materialistic.

It can also be said that working within this network of insincerity and deception is transubstantiation of Christs' body and blood into bread and wine for consumption. Although some would prefer to separate a people from their history, Greco-Roman acts of terror against humankind is evidence that transubstantiation is a form of symbolic cannibalism supporting a brutal world order of genocide, and ecocide dominated by European and Caucasian war technology.

An Emphasis on Physical Evolution

Miseducation concerning the origin and purpose of humankind also supports this current world order that celebrates physical power and domination in the forms of war and genocide. From the Eurocentric worldview and paradigm, evolution fathered by Charles Darwin developed into paleoanthropology, a branch of paleontology that focuses on humankind. Paleoanthropology seeks to understand the early development of anatomically modern humans through hominization. Evolutionary kinship lines within the family

Hominidae are reconstructed from the biological evidence of petrified skeletal remains, bone fragments, and footprints. Possible cultural evidence, stone tools, artifacts, and settlement localities are also used to establish lines of evolutionary kinship.

A possible intent of this Eurocentric emphasis on physical evolution is to identify the species solely with a less evolved human (Homo sapien) animal. To marginalize ancient people possessing civilizations that focus on a positive, spiritual existence in communion with nature, White supremacy continues to justify global domination through miseducation that favors Charles Darwin's physical evolution and paleoanthropology. Written into socio-religious text is a fear of, and aversion to spiritual evolution, given that the Sanhedrin council accused Jesus of blasphemy for claiming to be a son of God. A conclusion to this epic scripture and narrative is also physical crucifixion. The subliminal message for global populations might be to avoid physical torture and the crucifixion fate of Jesus, simply embrace the spiritual designation, and psychic limitations of sons and daughters of men, who conform to the established order. In other words, if Jesus were to conform to the Hebrew and Roman establishment by accepting the designation, and behaving as a son of man, not preaching personal and social change through spiritual liberation, he would not have suffered the physical and mental anguish of crucifixion. The Roman and Hebrew methods of social control were physical and psycho-spiritual torture, so that for their own preservation and salvation, Jesus and others would conform.

Chapter Nineteen

Sons and Daughters of Men Who Identify with Original Sin

An intent of fallacious socio-religious indoctrination may be to condition humankind to be sons and daughters of men, programmed to identify with uncontrollable, animalistic, innate-original sin. Socio-religious indoctrination may also condition the sons and daughters of men to accept negative emotionalism, and a lack of self-control as being human, acceptable, and normal. At its core, what is original sin? Could it be impulsive, less evolved, animalistic behaviors belonging to those lacking emotional control? If this is true, does indoctrination into the philosophy and lifestyle of original sin also create a pathway by which elitists, geopolitical leadership can control and manipulate the sons and daughters of men through implanted, impulsive emotionalism? Similarly, to maintain leadership positions, the clergy and other members of society are predisposed to quote socio-religious texts that condone juvenile and spiritually unevolved behaviors.

For instance, subliminally promoted as acceptable, Biblical King David desired another man's wife and motivated by jealousy, deployed her husband to die on the battlefield. According to Abrahamic tradition, King David emulated an attribute of a jealous and angry god. This embrace of jealousy is perhaps an anthropomorphic characterization of God, where humans place traits of negative emotionalism onto The Supreme Creator Being. It is therefore a reasonable conclusion that for the Abrahamic, negative human emotionalism is also acceptable, since it is an attribute of God. To feel vindicated, this perpetuates a web of entanglement permitting the sons and daughters of men to justify their own negativity. Within these narratives, accepted as godly and normal, also lies the pattern of labeling groups of people as evil and cursed devil worshippers, worthy of genocidal extermination.

Doctrine and teachings romanticizing original sin as acceptable in the forms of jealousy and negative emotionalism, likely encourages people to relinquish control of their lives, by trusting in Jesus. It is as though once accepting Christ as lord and savior, the miraculous holy spirit of faith and belief will grapple with unacknowledged negative emotionalism. Promoted, as well, is Christ's clergymen performing rituals and reciting supernatural prayers to set the captives free from sin, original or otherwise. Typically, regardless of lifestyle, clergymen are at the helm of ritualized leadership, where Biblical doctrine, and celebration through song, prayer, and praise are methods to cultivate clairvoyant powers that influence psychic, spiritual entities.

Clergymen are also allegedly adept at using socio-religious doctrine to influence spiritual forces to have either a positive or negative effect on peoples' behavior. Rarely mentioned is the impossibility for those who are negatively engaged in cultivating original sin to have a positive influence on spiritual entities, which results in a benevolent impact on congregants and the larger society. Nonetheless, Abrahamic traditions and clergy often support belief in influential entities, such as angels and demons that are powerful enough to manipulate humankind to commit genocide and ecocide. Naive and lacking sensibility are those who place their entire trust in the clergy. Regardless of negative or positive lifestyle choices, the clergy is thought to wield spiritual power to heal and set the captives free from original sin. On the subliminal level of spiritual practices, if the clergy's implicit (secret and hidden) lifestyle agenda is negative, instead of liberating and setting the captives free during rituals, the congregation will be pulled more deeply into original sin.

Negative Emotionalism

Other than Evangelicals, similar to White nationalists and supremacists, other Abrahamics reflect the doctrine and lifestyle of human original sin, by rationalizing and making excuses for genocidal behavior. Making excuses or blaming other people, or even supernatural entities, such as God and angels, or the devil and demons are attempts to shift accountability away from specific groups and individuals. The Eurocentric emphasis on human physical evolution and the Abrahamic, spiritual designation of inescapable original sin, denies empowerment through personal meditation, prayer, and rituals to regain accountability to their indwelling God, immediate family, and larger community. Although Abrahamics may say angelic, higher forms of life exist, others insist that the Christian saints and Jesus, along with his contingent of archangels are the only divine forms of life. Broadening this conversation to include all of God's infinite universe, most of which has never heard of Jesus, it becomes apparent that Christian saints, along with Christ himself and his cadre of angels, cannot be the only, highly evolved forms of spiritual life.

Some might argue that disobeying God is the original sin. The question remains, is there communion with, and adherence to the indwelling voice of God for those who identify with physical evolution, and are less concerned with spiritual progress and development? Negative emotionalism is original sin for those who engage in spiritual evolution through meditation, rituals, divination, and oracle use to elevate consciousness. Devotees of these practices cultivate eternal peace and joy (happiness), while in communion with, and adherence to the conscience, or indwelling voice of God. The conscience does not inform spiritually evolving beings to express negative emotionalism, which is a form of animalistic, original sin.

However, according to Biblical narratives, first Satan, or the devil in the form of a serpent is blamed for tempting Eve to eat a fruit from the tree of the knowledge of good and evil. Patriarchal, Biblical traditions are also biased against women. Founded on the sequence of events in the Garden of Eden, it is Eve who is most vulnerable to the devil's temptation. It is she who has conversations with the serpent, implying that the devil knew that Eve was susceptible to temptation to eat from the forbidden fruit. Not the devil, but Eve is blamed for offering and tempting Adam to eat from the fruit. Abrahamic traditions make it appear that the woman is the downfall of mankind. Biblical narratives also seem to portray Adam as an innocent bystander in this temptation event.

Chapter Twenty

Black Africans: The Original Anatomical and Spiritually Evolved Modern Humans (Homo sapien sapiens)

Along similar lines of discussion, others might say that religion, spirituality, history, and science are distinct disciplines that should not converge to form a holistic understanding of human origin and purpose. To the contrary, using genetics (DNA analysis) and anthropology, a holistic approach can be taken to research the origin of Adam and Eve. Using robust methodologies to analyze and compare fossilized remains, along with the genetics of ancient and modern humans, conclusive evidence supports that the first anatomical and spiritually evolved modern humans, or Homo sapien sapiens are Black Africans.

In 1987, Cann, Stoneking, and Wilson published a global survey of human mitochondrial DNA (mtDNA) in Nature magazine. The essential conclusion from this article was that all mtDNA stems from Black, African women who lived about

200,000 years ago. These African women, the ancestors of all modern humans (Homo sapien sapiens) have since been referred to as mitochondrial Eve. Mitochondria are little structures or organelles within the cell that are responsible for energy production. These organelles are different from other cell structures, since mitochondria contain their own DNA, separate from nuclear genetic material. MtDNA is also matrilineal, inherited only from mother to child. Regardless of gender, all DNA within the mitochondria was inherited from the mother.

In a 1987 study, researchers analyzed mtDNA samples from 147 different people, and discovered at least 133 distinct sequences within the genetic material. After comparing the number of variations among mtDNA samples from people with different racial or phenotypic characteristics, researchers found that Africans have the most distinctions compared to other groups of people. Compared to microbes, for example, humans have a much longer lifespan and reproduce less rapidly. Given this fact, it also takes longer for human DNA to undergo change, or express mutations. The group of humans who express the greatest mutated sequences in mtDNA are also the oldest, and most ancient people. The mtDNA of Black Africans reveal the greatest distinct, mutated sequences. Therefore, Black Africans are the oldest and original modern humans (Homo sapien sapiens), and mitochondrial Eve is their progenitor. The emphasis is not that only one woman gave rise to all of humankind. MtDNA analysis strongly supports that it was not a Caucasian, or Asian lineage that gave rise to all modern humans, but Black Africans, occasionally referred to as mitochondrial Eve. As the progenitors to anatomically and spiritually evolved modern humans, historical, anthropological, scientific, and archeological evidence supports that Black Africans constructed the highest forms of megalithic, spiritual civilization and culture in ancient Kemet.

Y Chromosome Adam: A Black African

A February 28, 2013, article in the American Journal of Human Genetics advances a new divergent Y chromosomal lineage, obtained from a contemporary Black man living in South Carolina. The African DNA lineage from this contemporary Black man branched from the Y chromosome tree before the first appearance of anatomically modern humans (Homo sapien sapiens) in the fossil record. Lab analysis indicates that this lineage diverged from previously known Y chromosomes about 338,000 years ago. Evidence suggests that anatomically modern humans had not yet evolved, at that time.

Originally, the DNA sample was submitted to the National Geographic Genographic Project. When none of the genetic markers used to assign lineages to known Y chromosome groupings were found, the sample was forwarded to Family Tree DNA, a company specializing in analysis to trace haplogroups and family origin, for further sequencing. This lab led the effort to analyze the genetic sequence, which includes more than 240,000 base pairs of the Y chromosome.

Unlike chromosomes that determine physical characteristics, most genes on the Y-sex chromosome do not exchange DNA with autosomal genetic material. This lack of crossing over, or transpositioning of genes on the Y chromosome, makes it less difficult to trace ancestral relationships among contemporary lineages. Two individuals carrying the same Y chromosome mutation suggests that they share a common paternal ancestor. Similar to African Eve with multiple mtDNA variations, Y chromosome mutations that are not dominant in broader populations, indicate inheritance from an older common ancestor.

Michael Hammer, associate professor from the University of Arizona's research lab says, the newly discovered Y chromosome variation is extremely rare. Through large database searches, Mr. Hammer's team of investigators were eventually able to uncover a similar chromosome variant in the Mbo population of Western Cameroon in sub-Saharan Africa. Traditional Twa, the Khoi and San or Khoi-San people are also considered among the most diverged human populations living today.

Fossil record evidence, along with genetic material from the lineages of mitochondrial Eve and Y chromosome Adam definitively points to Black Africans being the original, anatomically and spiritually evolved modern humans (Homo sapien sapiens). Evidence from contemporary DNA analysis also demonstrates that Black Africans interbred with their older cousins (Homo sapiens), such as Neanderthals, Denisovans, and Homo floresiensis. It was this interbreeding that produced people with different phenotypic characteristics. Black Africans who remained on the continent and did not migrate tend to have minuscule amounts of Neanderthal, Denisovan, or Homo floresiensis genes, which lives on in contemporary modern humans carrying the Caucasian and Asian phenotype. Genes from archaic cousins helped Black Africans to adapt to new environmental conditions, but it may also inhibit spiritual evolution.

Chapter Twenty-one

The Daughters and Sons of God: The Paut Neteru and Metu Neter

To transition from original sin and the sons and daughters of men, into forms of evolution or revolution and liberation belonging to the daughters and sons of God, the spiritual anatomy of humankind should be studied, understood, and lived. The sacred geometrical platform onto which the Paut Neteru (Tree of Life) is constructed, makes possible an integral understanding of natural, archetypal personalities and energies that flow through, and reside within humankind. The Paut Neteru system elucidates the spiritual anatomy of mankind to provide maneuverability through life's challenges, while transitioning into higher states of consciousness and understanding.

The Metu Neter series authored by Ra Un Nefer Amen provides comprehensive, detailed explanations of the Paut Neteru: The sacred geometrical framework illustrating the spiritual anatomy of humankind. The Metu Neter series substantiates the Paut Neteru by presenting a cosmological architecture that expounds the creation of the universe, including the different levels or stages of mankind's spiritual evolution and development. Foundational to living the Paut Neteru and Metu Neter teachings and philosophies is acknowledging The Creator's consciousness as the support structure for all entities in existence. In the beginning, 13.9 billion-years-ago, there was only God's consciousness and everything in existence was, then, placed into this framework. In simple terms, God's consciousness is scaffolded into scientific, mathematical principles and laws governing the universe. Detailed and robust research to explain the structural and organizational levels of quarks, bosons, electrons, and other subatomic particles are also elemental constituents within the Paut Neteru and Metu Neter.

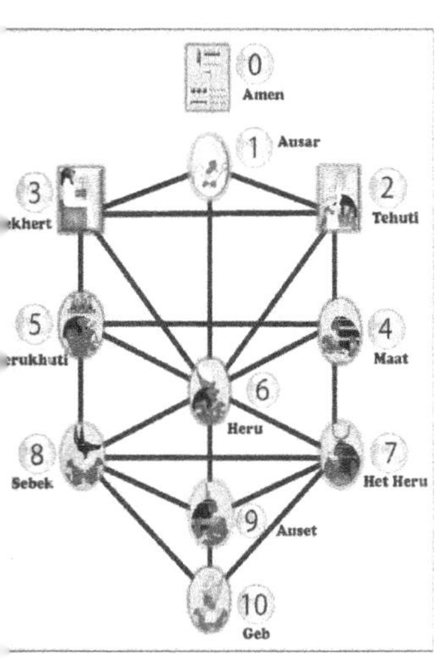

As the honorable Ra Un Nefer Amen describes creation, and the eternal procession from God's conscious awareness, to energy, then matter, he says: "In the lower half of Ashiah is where we find the atomic, and molecular organization of physical matter." The origin of God's 13.9 billion years of conscious awareness is also referred to as a singularity, the void, nothingness, the subjective realm, or pure consciousness. To clarify Dr. Amen's description, a simplified version of the atomic structure can be utilized. God's pure and undifferentiated consciousness or awareness is the original particle that guides and directs all things, or matter in the objective realm to come into existence. As Dr. Amen mentions ". . . [the] molecular organization of physical matter", a model of a hydrogen atom can be utilized. Hydrogen is the simplest of elements, and its electron is the energy particle that orbits the core, containing a proton, but lacking a neutron. It is God's conscious awareness that is the directional guide, stabilizing this atomic configuration, and all things in the universe. This teachable atomic model also becomes a moment to emphasize that opposites attract. The negatively charged electron, or energy particle, is attracted to the positively charged core, containing the proton. If not for this balanced arrangement of attraction, the electron would be propelled from the orbit of the atomic core into outer space.

Divisions of the Spirit

For some, spirit is also described as an energy component. As Dr. Amen explains: "The part of the spirit dwelling on this plane (Ashiah) is the well-known physical body, which is called the Khab by the Kemetians, and Guph by the Canaanites." To clarify, the physical body referred to as the Khab or Guph is a denser manifestation of the spirit. Energy (spirit) is also defined as the ability to do work. With all elements, there is the core with its protons and neutrons, comprising the atomic mass (weight). In addition, matter is defined as anything that has mass and takes up space in a container. From the previously described subatomic structure, and now to the macroscopic level of human existence, the container is the physical body, vessel, or vehicle.

Still using this simplified atomic model to explain life on this physical plane of existence, it can be said that spirit (energy), similar to the electron, is attracted to physical matter (the core of the atom). The spirit (energy and ability to do work) is attached or attracted to matter (the physical body), so that mankind can function and achieve purpose. Dr. Amen goes on to say: "It must be noted that in traditional African metaphysics, there is no distinction made between the physical, and man's higher bodies. The physical body is considered an integral part of the spirit, its densest component." In other words, the less dense, energy component (spirit) of mankind is capable of transcending to high states of conscious existence, even though confined, attached, or attracted to the physical body, its most dense core.

On the sacred, geometrical lattice and framework of the Paut Neteru (Tree of Life), Geb (sphere 10) is at the rung, or step representing the densest level of spiritual existence. The planet Earth, including physical matter, bodies, vessels, or vehicles on this plane of existence can be symbolized by Geb. Within Geb (sphere 10) on the Paut Neteru, there are the Khab, and the Khaibit divisions of the spirit. According to Dr. Amen, the Khab (7th division): Houses man's physical body, composed of atoms and subatomic particles. The physical body is also referred to as the animal body, and this is linked to paleoanthropology, and physical evolution of the human. As stated by Dr. Amen, ". . . it is at the level of the Khab that each previous manifestation is finally segregated into an individual existence." Seemingly, there is progressive differentiation and distinctions from prior phenomena, resulting in the formation of the Khab division. Quarks, bosons, atoms, and molecules that were once segregated, now congeal into a physical body that can function in this fourth dimensional reality of time and space.

For simplicity, these progressions seem to be linear, but they are not. A multitude of occurrences all happen at the same time. Electrons (energy component and spirit of atoms) are shared or exchanged during bond formation, so that larger molecules and compounds can manifest into physical matter that include bodies, vessels, and vehicles. In linear progression, and on the most elemental levels, the physical components of a body are not yet animate or energized until integration of the Khaibit (6th division). As stated by Dr. Amen, the Khaibit is the motive power of being. It is the life force, the animal spirit, the emotions, and sensations. In addition, the Khaibit houses man's life force: Qi, Kundalini, or animal soul. It is at the 6th division of the spirit that each substance receives its breath of life, if alive and animate.

On the cellular level, animate objects or organisms exchange gases utilizing the breath of life for energy production, and homeostasis (health or balance). For aerobes, the breath of life is oxygen containing air, which allows for enhanced energy (spirit or ATP) production. In different forms, photosynthetic organisms and anaerobes also utilize gases or the breath of life to maintain an ecological balance. Dr. Amen also says: "The electromagnetic motive force (if non-living), enables inanimate objects to act upon the physical plane." Both animate and inanimate objects rely on the electromagnetic motive force. For cellular communication that regulates homeostasis in complex-multicellular organisms, an action potential should accumulate to generate an electromagnetic impulse that can cause the release of nerve-cell neurotransmitters. With inanimate objects including artificial-electronic devices, an electromagnetic field is generated that can interfere, or disrupt communication among animate cells, comprising complex-multicellular organisms The ancients were much more mindful and adept at projecting their biological energy field to commingle with Earth's physical and natural Khabit, to amplify spirit to support interactions and communication between the daughters and sons of God and higher forms of angelic beings (the Shepsu and Neteru).

Chapter Twenty-two

The Sahu and Ab Divisions of the Spirit

The 5th division of the spirit (Sahu), houses man's intellect including the human soul, the mind's storehouse of self-knowledge. Within Sahu there are three faculties: 9 (Auset), 8 (Sebek), and 7 (Hetheru). The Paut Neteru, illustrates a synthesis or integration of the divisions of the spirit with that of primordial, archetypal personality characteristics that reflect African ancestry, through the forces of nature (the Neteru), speaking directly to mankind's spiritual evolution, development, and power, or lack thereof. For some, the Paut Neteru may suggest a theoretical framework, but for others, it is a realistic and functional apparatus that enables humankind to speak a spiritual language, while living its reality. Dr. Amen describes *the specializing organs of Being*, as codified within Sahu, which includes faculties 9, 8, and 7. From inception, as mankind continues to evolve into a human soul with an intellect, a storehouse for the mind develops, and awareness of self begins to take shape. It is within these faculties and the Sahu division that the human mind and spirit individualizes into a separate and distinct existence, functioning within social units, such as a family group.

The 4th division of the spirit (Ab) is *the administrative organs of Being*, or the vehicle from which the self manifests. In the previous division (Sahu), awareness of self (the true essence of Being) is beginning to emerge. Whether conscious or subconscious, occurring within humankind is the process of transitioning through the divisions of the spirit to activate or manifest the self. Whether the self (the true essence of Being) continues to be nourished through birth, as it transitions onto this physical plane of existence (Geb) is dependent on lifestyle choices, and societal interaction. In other words, information about, and continued nourishment (prayer, meditation, yoga, Qi Gong) and other rituals to enhance actualization of self, are dependent on the group dynamic, and institutionalized social norms into which the individual is born or incarnated.

In the Ab division, the self begins to manifest, or is actualized and starts to function. Within the Ab there are faculty 6 (Heru), faculty 5 (Herukhuti), and faculty 4 (Maat). Dr. Amen asserts: Once the manifestations are set in motion by the three preceding divisions, Sahu (5), Khaibit (6) and Khab (7), the fourth division of the spirit (Ab) programs scientific principles and laws into the Being, enabling it to function as a cohesive whole, not in violation with itself, which includes its other divisions and faculties. Dr. Amen also says that as far as the spiritual, evolutionary stage of most humans: "Man is in the Ab and Sahu divisions of spiritual development. They are what goes through the judgement."

Based on daily behavior, most of mankind functions out of the Ab and Sahu divisions of the spirit. Again, whether the human is aware or not, a nightly soliloquy with the indwelling God, the conscience, occurs. These faculties and divisions of the spirit are natal and inborn. They are the spiritual anatomy of humankind. From birth, to functioning on Geb, this physical plane of existence, mankind knows proper and correct behavior, since this, too, is programmed into the spirit. The human has the freedom to choose. The choice, however, is often to violate its own innate (natural), spiritual programming. This innate and correct programming is similar to forms of instinct that function within the animal and plant kingdoms. The human chooses to violate the self (the true essence of Being). Hence the nightly judgement of the heart that may be weighed down by human violations, resulting in inhibitions from experiencing divine-spiritual liberation. This is analogous to a bird that has weights on its feet, but is expected to fly and soar through the heavens.

Chapter Twenty-three

The Shekhem, Khu and Ba Divisions of the Spirit

The Ab division of the spirit incorporates 3 faculties: (6) Heru, (5) Herukhuti, and (4) Maat. As mentioned previously, Sahu is made up of 3 faculties as well: (7) Hetheru, (8) Sebek, and (9) Auset. These two divisions of the spirit: The Ab and Sahu are the repository for the faculties of man, which include the human, or the sons and daughters of man. The Shekhem or the 3rd division of the spirit is integrated into the 3rd faculty on the Paut Neteru, which is also referred to as Sekher(t). This 3rd division and faculty houses man's ability to manifest spiritual power and to share God's power. It is this sharing of God's spiritual power to manifest goodness, mercy, and love into the world that distinguishes the daughters and sons of God.

The 2nd division is the Khu, which houses man's wisdom faculty and ability to receive direct guidance from God. The Khu (2nd division) is expressed through the cultivation and manifestation of wisdom that corresponds to Tehuti: The second faculty on the Paut Neteru. Dr. Amen states that the

Kemetic words, Metu Neter, translates into the word of God. The teachings, philosophies, and positive spiritual lifestyle of the Metu Neter and Paut Neteru are integral to nurturing and developing the intuitive faculty through mediation, trance induction, and oracle use to receive direct guidance from God. Dr. Amen also says that the 2nd (Khu) and 3rd (Shekhem) divisions are *the creative organs of Being*.

He clarifies by saying: Khu is the divine Will, and on this level of functionality, there is direct, two-way communication between initiates and God. The initiate processes communicated information and chooses to adhere and follow divine Will: The imagery, words, and directions from God. By adhering to divine Will, spiritual power through the Sekher(t) faculty and Shekhem division are activated, accentuated, and realized. In combination, the Khu and Shekhem are *the creative organs of Being*, because divine women and men implement God's Will to create a peaceful, harmonious abode here on Earth. Dr. Amen adds: "Note that while the Will (Khu) is the faculty of potential action, the Spiritual Power (Shekhem) is the vehicle for the actualization of the actions." The Khu division is the potential, since man has the will to choose to follow, or not to adhere to truth and wisdom. To transition from sons and daughters of men into daughters and sons of God, adhere and follow divine Will (Khu) to activate, realize, and live spiritual power through the Sheker(t) faculty and Shekhem division.

The 1st division of the spirit is the Ba. On the Paut Neteru, the Ba division corresponds to Ausar (1st faculty). As Dr. Amen affirms: The Ba is *The seat of Consciousness and Identity*. Consciousness can be defined as functional awareness that exists even within inanimate objects. Some would say that atoms and subatomic particles are inanimate, but based on scientific principles and laws, particles also have a conscious awareness, informing and guiding them to bond by exchanging or sharing electrons. Others would say that this consciousness stems from the The Supreme Creator Being (Nebertcher), the foundational fabric of the universe, holding all things in balance and proper orientation.

The Ba division of the spirit is that natal, divine, inborn consciousness originating from God. Wholeness, peace, and tranquility can be experienced through the breath: the gateway between the voluntary Will (Heru) and the autonomic nervous system or subconscious domain of Ausar. The internal, exemplary, and exquisite model that can be aroused, and resurrected through meditation, ritual, and hekau (words and sounds of power) to manifest spiritually evolved behavior also represents Ausar. Dr. Amen describes the Ba as: *The true ego of Being.* Daughters and sons of God identify with their divine Self: the indwelling Ba of Ausar and the ability to experience and express oneness with God, residing in all existence.

The Ba is "the true residence of the Self" according to Dr. Amen. He also expounds, the divine spirit comprises three divisions: The Ba (1), Khu (2), and Shekhem (3). Not known to the sons and daughters of men, socio-religious and miseducational programming and conditioning can confine the spirit to the Ab and Sahu divisions. However, these designations provide men with a functional existence on this physical plane, since Ab (4), is the vehicle of self-manifestation. The Sahu (3) is the mind's storehouse of self-knowledge: human or divine. As knowledge from life experiences are stored in the mind, the self begins to manifest, but sons and daughters of men may choose to continue to identify with a human, limited to the Ab and Sahu divisions of the spirit. Alternatively, the human can choose to identify with the divine and aspire to be Ausar. In which case, spiritual work is fulfilled to provide for a transition to the Shekhem (3), Khu (2), and Ba (1) divisions.

Conclusion

The empirical emphasis on physical evolution functions to limit the sons and daughters of men to the level of warmongering animals, controlled by fear. Strategies to indoctrinate fear into mass populations are coded within Abrahamic messages of God's jealous wrath and eternal damnation to hell. In America, mass media is used to message fear-based political rhetoric that speaks to White constituents, notifying them that Latinx, migrant-gang members, and Black, low-income rioters are invading their country and suburbs. Abrahamic indoctrination works hand-in-glove with government and corporate disinformation, miseducation, and propaganda to control the sons and daughters of men, who are not seeking spiritual liberation, but are fearful of losing physical possessions and property.

Daughters and sons of God are those receptive to the urgency of spiritual evolution, through continued aspirations to engage in yoga, meditation, ritual, Qi Gong, oracle readings, prayer, etc. Intrinsic, ancestral experiences encoded in DNA bring the daughters and sons of God to the realization that fear does not liberate, but confines the spirit to limited-empirical reality. With the first coming of Jesus, roughly 2,021 years ago, that savior was crucified for disseminating radical messages of spiritual liberation. Since then, for approximately 2,000 years governments, corporations, and socio-religious institutions have confined the sons and daughters of men to a fear-based, empirical reality contrary to the lifestyle, philosophy, and teachings of Christ. On August 28th, 2020, the 57th anniversary of the historic march on Washington, Martin

Luther King Junior III, gave a speech on the steps of the Lincoln Memorial to a contingent of 70,000 spectators and participants for social justice. In that speech, Martin Luther King Junior III charged the gathering to "save themselves" from this protracted tide of social and racial injustice. The August 28th Commitment March on Washington was organized and facilitated by Rev Al Sharpton and his National Action Network.

From this most poignant speech, a resounding message is that there is no departed savior, who has embarked on a journey to save mankind from itself. Humankind should not be passive and inactive, but instead intercept social injustice, where it hides in the mental enclave of people harboring deceitful and putrefied duplicity. In contrast, those who celebrate this present moment will abandon outdated, socio-religious anticipation of the second coming of Christ. Continued engagement of consciousness elevation practices will resurrect and cause the rebirth of the daughters and sons of God, who realize that they are shareholders in their own salvation and redemption: The third coming of spiritual liberation.

BIBLIOGRAPY TO CHAPTERS

Chapter One

1. Lee, Felicia. "From Noah's Curse to Slavery's Rationale." The New York Times, 1 Nov. 2003, www.nytimes.com/2003/11/01/arts/from-noah-s-curse-to-slavery-s-rationale.html.

2. Fredrickson, George, and Albert Camarillo. Racism: A Short History (Princeton Classics, 106). Revised, Princeton University Press, 2015.

Chapter Two

1. "What Is Qi Gong? Taoist Master Explains Power of Qi and Philosophy." YouTube, uploaded by George Thompson, 26 Nov. 2020, www.youtube.com/watch?v=bsJRGT3d0DU.

2. "�9 Ankh Udja Seneb �4 Hekau | Kemetic Chant for Prosperity in 2020." YouTube, uploaded by Kemetic Wellness – BaNAuset KaNSekhmet, BSN, RN, 1 Jan. 2020, www.youtube.com/watch?v=ClYZTDvFaA8&t=3s

Chapter Three

1. "Citizens United Threatens Democracy." The Billings Gazette [Montana], May 2017, billingsgazette.com/news/opinion/mailbag/citizens-united-threatens-democracy/article_f6564917-3d24-5461-a8f6-c320a143f1d6.html.

2. "The Birth of a Nation - Full Movie - (1915) HD - The Masterpiece of Racist Cinema." YouTube, uploaded by Khalbrae, 1 Aug. 2015, www.youtube.com/watch?v=ebtiJH3EOHo.

3. "The Impact of FLUORIDE on the Developing Brain." YouTube, uploaded by The Impact of FLUORIDE on the Developing Brain, 7 Oct. 2020, www.youtube.com/watch?v=hI4kpvW760M

4. "Super Fly T.N.T. (1973) | Directed by Ron 'O Neal #ShielaFrazierWeek." YouTube, uploaded by reelblack, 29 Oct. 2019, www.youtube.com/watch?v=4M6AYLoNc7c.

Chapter Four

1. "How an Artificial Sweetener May Have Destroyed the Roman Empire." YouTube, uploaded by Weird History, 4 Nov. 2020, www.youtube.com/watch?v=A1bLGQ4E8D0.

2. "Why Did the Roman Empire Fall?" YouTube, uploaded by Florida PASS Program, 10 Aug. 2016, www.youtube.com/watch?v=pcWoR9i-GvA.

Chapter Five

1. "How Christianity Spread in Rome - Secrets Of Christianity 105 - Selling Christianity." YouTube, uploaded by TOP BOX TV, 24 Sept. 2019, www.youtube.com/watch?v=S7A7-KOFyMA.

2. French, Kerrie. "Constantine's Creation of Jesus Christ." The Council of Nicaea, 2017, outlawjimmy.com/wp-content/uploads/2017/10/Constantines-Creation-Of-Jesus-Christ.pdf.

Chapter Six

1. "MITHRAEUM." MITHRAEUM, 2015, mithraeum.info.

Chapter Seven

1. "History of Christianity: How Christianity Was Invented." YouTube, uploaded by Pryupism, 24 Feb. 2017, www.youtube.com/watch?v=6f_8Z7fxfIY.

Chapter Eight

1. "Superhumans: The Remarkable Brain Waves of High-Level Meditators | Daniel Goleman | Big Think." YouTube, uploaded by Florida PASS Program, 13 Sept. 2018, www.youtube.com/watch?v=10J6crRacZg.

Chapter Nine

1. "DR. QUANTUM - DOUBLE SLIT EXPERIMENT." YouTube, uploaded by Angel Art, 27 Dec. 2010, www.youtube.com/watch?v=Q1YqgPAtzho.

2. Cremo, Michael. The Forbidden Archeologist by Michael Cremo. Michael Cremo, 2018.

3. Amen, Ra Un Nefer. Metu Neter: The Great Oracle of Tehuti and the Egyptian System of Spiritual Cultivation. Vol. 1, Ra Un Nefer Amen, 1990.

Chapter Ten

1. "Cognitive Dissonance (Definition + 3 Examples)." YouTube, uploaded by Practical Psychology, 12 Apr. 2021, www.youtube.com/watch?v=G1-vaIe2FGM.

2. "What Is Māyā?" YouTube, uploaded by Embodied Philosophy, 12 Feb. 2020, www.youtube.com/watch?v=I-WzGwe-BRo.

Chapter Eleven

1. Egyptian Dawn: Exposing the Real Truth Behind Ancient Egypt. 0 ed., London, England, Random House, 2010.

Chapter Twelve

1. Hitti, Natashah. "Elon Musk's Neuralink Implant Will 'Merge' Humans with AI." Dezeen, 25 May 2021, www.dezeen.com/2019/07/22/elon-musk-neuralink-implant-ai-technology.

2. "Dr. Judy Wood: 'Evidence of Breakthrough Energy on 9/11' | Www.Kla.Tv." YouTube, uploaded by Klagemauer TV - English, 11 Sept. 2018, www.youtube.com/watch?v=bRq2xQSPPJk.

Chapter Thirteen

1. Darwin, Charles. The Descent of Man. Digireads.com Publishing, 2019.

2. Kipling, Rudyard. The Five Nations (The Writings in Prose and Verse of Rudyard Kipling. Outward Bound Edition. Book 21). Wentworth Press, 2019.

Chapter Fourteen

1. "Darwinian Evolution and Racism with Ken Ham." YouTube, uploaded by Answers in Genesis, 7 Aug. 2018, www.youtube.com/watch?v=kIqjpPZ0-es.

2. "Native Americans and Manifest Destiny." YouTube, uploaded by Emily Payne, 30 Apr. 2018, www.youtube.com/watch?v=tiCUN209hWw.

Chapter Fifteen

1. "Exploring The Astonishing Osiris Shaft On The Giza Plateau." YouTube, uploaded by ORLANDO FUORIOSO, 2 July 2019, www.youtube.com/watch?v=Rtk4QeB6vjk.

Chapter Sixteen

1. Ehrman, Bart. How Jesus Became God: The Exaltation of a Jewish Preacher from Galilee. Annotated, HarperOne, 2021.

Chapter Seventeen

1. "Why Study Arius of Alexandria with Mary Cunningham." YouTube, uploaded by University of Nottingham, 6 May 2015, www.youtube.com/watch?v=5syHIRQvLaw.

Chapter Eighteen

1. "Nicene Creed with Historic Intro." YouTube, uploaded by cool.seminary.tutorials, 17 Mar. 2020, www.youtube.com/watch?v=iKSujlKlLr8.

Chapter Nineteen

1. "5 Minute Guided Meditation to Release Negative Thoughts and Emotions | Mindfulness Practice." YouTube, uploaded by Soul and Sage, 20 Nov. 2020, www.youtube.com/watch?v=5CIr_FBW4hE.

Chapter Twenty

1. "'Mitochondrial DNA and Human Evolution' (1987), by Rebecca Louise Cann, Mark Stoneking, and Allan Charles Wilson | The Embryo Project Encyclopedia." The Embryo Project Encyclopedia, 2014, embryo.asu.edu/pages/mitochondrial-dna-and-human-evolution-1987-rebecca-louise-cann-mark-stoneking-and-allan.

2. "Study Says Oldest Known Human Y-Chromosome Branch Dates to 338,000 Years Ago | Genetics | Sci-News.Com." Breaking Science News | Sci-News.Com, 2013, www.sci-news.com/genetics/article00915.html.

Chapter Twenty-One

1. "Ra Un Nefer Amen - The Kemetic Tree of Life Pt 7 of 12." YouTube, uploaded by Ancestral Productions, 29 July 2016, www.youtube.com/watch?v=NG7e9jG7pmg.